LIVING FULLY

WITH

LOW VISION

AND

BLINDNESS

TED LENNOX
EDITOR: NINA DERDA

Order this book online at www.trafford.com
or email orders@trafford.com

Most Trafford titles are also available at major online book retailers.

Printed in the United States of America.

ISBN: 978-1-4669-1570-1 (sc)
ISBN: 978-1-4669-1572-5 (hc)
ISBN: 978-1-4669-1571-8 (e)

Library of Congress Control Number: 2012903180

Trafford rev. 03/15/2012

 www.trafford.com

North America & international
toll-free: 1 888 232 4444 (USA & Canada)
phone: 250 383 6864 ♦ fax: 812 355 4082

TABLE OF CONTENTS

PREFACE

If you question what this book is all about, let me explain. The main theme of the book deals with ideas, notions, and suggestions for ways to live effectively with low vision or blindness. Many of the ideas expressed are about living in general and could apply to anyone.

Now here's an important paragraph. The words, thoughts, and ideas included in this book are in no way meant to tell you, the reader, what to do and how to live. Above all, I would encourage you to think for yourself. That is, whatever I suggest is only that—a suggestion. You decide whether it is appropriate for you. Please do your own thinking and do not let me, or anyone else, control your thinking, acting, and living.

Taking the above paragraph just a bit further, you will note throughout the book that I include stories and comments about myself. Many of these stories and comments indicate that I would do better if I could go back in time. But, doesn't that say something about others and probably me? I think it a good idea to keep improving one's life. That is emphasized throughout the book.

There are thirteen chapters in this book. Each chapter title provides information about the subjects in the chapter. Chapter 13 is a broad summary of the first twelve chapters. Therefore, if you wish, you could skip to Chapter 13 and find out a great deal about what's included in the book.

I start each chapter with a brief preview of what will be covered. This is followed by the content itself and a short summary of what has been presented. In addition, there are two other things in the chapters. You will find my poetry in some. The reasons are:

- I find that in a few words, poetry can say a great deal.
- I personally enjoy poetry. Thus, by my including poetry, you will get to know me a little better.

Also in each chapter, I end with a little humor-either a brainteaser, riddle or joke. That is because I think that challenging the brain, and laughing, is important and fun. You'll note that I end Chapter 12 with a short section on "Make Learning Fun. Make Life Fun"!

Finally, if you have any comments or thoughts, do not hesitate to send me an e-mail. I will definitely reply. When sending a message to my e-mail address, please use the following in the Subject line: "Response to Chapter __"

Please enjoy the book, and as emphasized above, and throughout the book, I am not telling anyone what to do or what to think. If there were an underlying theme in this book, it would be that you are being encouraged to think for yourself and to be an unlimited, unique person. The following poem helps us to "SET NO LIMITS". It is taken from my book, **DIE DAILY: Dream, Improve, Enjoy.**

SET NO LIMITS

I have something so important to say,
This message especially I want to convey.
At birth we are all given a brain,
It is crucial for us to train our brain!

Many people influence our mind,
Often unknowingly they are unkind.
We allow a fence around our mind to erect,
That fence, it may have a powerful effect!

Too often a seed in us they plant,
That seed is known, as "I can't."
Limits we place on ourselves: that's sad,
Is there anything that could be worse?

Think of our mind as a garden growing,
Each day it could stand a little hoeing.
Let's clear out every single weed,
Fertilize it with positive thoughts, indeed!

Let me state my case real plain-
We are taught to place limits on our brain.
We're not good at math, music, or art,
We learn these beliefs almost from the start!

Now here's another way to train your brain,
You are limitless is my refrain.
Please, my friend, do not limits set,
Limitless you are, on that you can bet!

How do you teach yourself this wonderful notion?
This should be a lifelong devotion.
Program yourself to believe this thought,
Over-ride every negative belief you've been taught!

There are techniques I'd like to share
Because for me and for you, I care.
This is a poem and I hope you'll keep reading,
Considering my thoughts and my sincere pleading.

Let me suggest just one simple technique,
Maybe to your heart it just may speak.
Three times each day I'd like to suggest,
I think I too will follow this request.

Here we go with this Powerful thought,
"I am unlimited," despite what I've been taught.

That's just nine words every twenty-four hours,
Do it for a month and enjoy your new powers!

Teach yourself about your unlimited brain.
I hope I don't bore you with this repeated refrain.
"I am unlimited," this thought you need to believe,
Then off you go to live and achieve!

ACKNOWLEDGEMENTS

I want to acknowledge and thank five important people who assisted me in the writing of this book. Their names are Nina Derda, Dennis Opoka, Nancy Kimberlin, Gloria and Bob Wurdock. In each case I will tell you about their role in my book, and then, because they are really wonderful people, I will make them real by telling you just one story in which they and I were part. Thus:

Nina Derda

My wife Laura and I have been friends with Nina and Ed for the past 41 years. Nina carefully read and typed this book and made suggestions and improvements. Further, her encouragement and her support have been motivating for me. Now to just one marvelous memory!

Nina and I have been running together for the past 29 years. This episode occurred in January of 1984. One Saturday morning we drove to Hell, Michigan, to participate in their winter 10 K Run called "When Hell Freezes Over!" The temperature was 5 degrees above zero. We were standing at the starting line ready for the race to begin. A kind gentleman to my left (Nina was on my right) calmly said:

"Tell your wife that you both need to be careful on the roads. There is plenty of ice and snow out there."

With nothing but joy in my heart and a huge smile on my face (I'm smiling now as I write this) I said:

"My wife is sitting in our living room, sipping her coffee, and reading the newspaper."

Dennis Opoka

Dennis read this book chapter by chapter. After reading he gave me his valuable feedback and suggestions. His thoughts were so helpful.

On November 2, 1956, I started my teaching job. I walked into our classroom and my friend Ralph Peabody introduced me to a little seven year old. His name was Dennis Opoka. Thus, Dennis was the very first student that I met. At the time I had no idea that he would be involved in this book. Just think-that was 55 years ago.

I could probably write an entire book about Nina and Dennis, so let me stop here and move on. However, here's a question for you! How can I stop here and yet move on?!

Nancy Kimberlin

Chapter 7 has three drawings. They are tactile drawings, and they demonstrate how different tactile drawings are from visual drawings. My friend Nancy Kimberlin is a motivated and wonderful artist. She has taken the tactile drawings of a football field, bowling lane, and baseball diamond and converted them to visual drawings. In this case the visual drawings are duplicates of the tactile drawings. Nancy has enhanced the meaning of touch pictures in Chapter 7. I am so grateful to her because the concepts in Chapter 7 are so important.

I developed a warm friendship with Nancy four years ago when she did three exciting drawings for my first book DIE DAILY. The drawings are in Chapter Five, "I Don't Mind Being Blind". In Chapter 5, Nancy has made three pictures to illustrate three poems:

One poem is called "Braille Is Beautiful". The print drawing is of the Braille dots.

The second poem is "To Bed We Go". The picture shows my wife and I in bed. She has the light on and is reading a book, while I am sleeping away.

Then, there is a poem and a drawing of a restroom, to amplify the notion of how restrooms are different.

Gloria and Bob Wurdock

Gloria and Bob Wurdock reviewed and proofread this book. They added much quality to the manuscript. That is, they helped improve the clarity of the book and in many instances improved the punctuation and formatting. I am so appreciative for their encouragement, positive ideas, and support.

Gloria, Bob, and I have been playing Braille Scrabble now for a couple of years. Last night we had a thrilling game. One play before the end, Bob was leading Gloria 151 to 145. Gloria went out, making her the final player. Her score was 150. Bob had to subtract two points from his score because of the number of points remaining in his tray. Thus, Gloria won 150-149. I was third with 145. Our games are always filled with fun.

So, Nina, Dennis, Nancy, Bob and Gloria, many thanks to each of you. I must end this part of my book now, for I am on my way to spend the evening with Gloria and Bob. We will be playing another lively and fun-filled Scrabble game.

INTERESTING WORDS

Following is a list of words that I am defining to be sure that I am communicating with you. First, I like words and I like playing with them. It is just plain fun for me. Second, the words in this list are ones I seldom use; perhaps they are not familiar to some of you.

COGITATE: To think about something.

COGNIZANT: To be aware of or to know about something.

CONGLOMERATION: A collection of related items.

CONJECTURING: Guessing.

DIGRESS: To temporarily leave the main topic, but to return shortly.

ELUCIDATE: To explain something further.

EUPHORIA: A state of being happy and enthused.

REITERATE: To repeat something already stated.

CHAPTER 1

THE AUTHOR

Read this book if you dare
As you read try to care

The following poem is from <u>DIE DAILY</u>, the book I authored in 2009. It is a poetic introduction of me, and hopefully it will give you a glimpse into my life.

SNEAK A PEEK

I popped into the world in 1933.
Born in the back of our drugstore—please believe me.
Since then, and right up to now, part of my life's scheme
Is that I enjoy and relish eating ice cream!

At age five, my family I left,
My heart, my heart it became bereft.
Back in those days if you could not see,
You left home and to school you had to flee.

While in school I participated in many a sport,
Baseball, basketball, football, and more I'm happy to report,
At Michigan State I wrestled, I was not great.
One hundred fifty seven was my wrestling weight.

Thanks to my good friends Ralph and Del,
I had a teaching career that was oh so swell.
Forty-eight years was my career's duration,
Every day was a wonderful sensation.

It was at Michigan State I met my wife Laura,
During college—a degree, a wife, who could ask for more?
My wife Laura I simply adore,
Living with her life could not be a bore!

Marla and Amy are our daughters supreme,
For both Laura and I they fulfilled our dream.
They've added to our life a special note,
Marla and Amy, you get our vote.

When you read this book please don't hesitate,
A message from you would be so great!
I promise I will reply within a week.
Thanks for taking this little peek!

One of the purposes of this book is to encourage you to create yourself by doing your own thinking, following your own path, and not being under anyone else's control. The picture I have in mind is that I am talking personally with you, the reader. Think of us sitting together engaged in a discussion, exchanging thoughts. At no point am I telling you what to think or what to do. I am sharing ideas with the hope that you will live a fruitful and limitless life. I want to share some of my experiences with you, and also my thoughts, feelings and perceptions as I strive to be happy, peaceful and confident.

When you are creating yourself, you are in charge of your Self-talk (what you say to yourself), you are expressing your uniqueness, and you are finding joy and fulfillment moment by moment. My aim in sharing my experiences is to help, encourage, and stimulate each person to be proud of themselves and their attributes. They should never be ashamed of their height, their gender, or being blind. The key is to always be proud of who you are. Two concepts which I will discuss that can help achieve that are Self-talk and dreams. I invite you to read this book with an open mind and an adventurous attitude.

Throughout my adult life I was a teacher. Those wonderful years were spent teaching blind and visually impaired elementary school children. For a four-year period I had youngsters with varying challenges. Some had cerebral palsy, some had hearing problems, some mobility limits, and some had low or no vision.

During the last twenty years my students called me "Mr. OBG"—old, bald and gray. I responded by referring to myself as "Mr. Young and Handsome." I leave that decision to anyone else. In my final year I had the privilege of teaching computer technology at the high school to my former elementary school youngsters. What a thrill it was to be back with those students who were now 16 and 17 years old.

I can't say I worked as a teacher, because basically I played every day. My students and co-workers were such a joy! Thus, my career seemed very short. I retired after only 47.6 years.

Chapter Summary

I have introduced myself and stated the aim and purpose of this book. In poetic form, the essence of the chapter is:

Set no limits on your life!
Live with joy and not with strife!

Chapter Humor

About ten days before Thanksgiving a farmer was standing in his field with white cane in hand. There were over one hundred turkeys walking about making sounds—but not "Gobble, gobble". Their sounds were "Moo, moo", pretending to be cows. Smart turkeys, I'd say.

CHAPTER 2

BE PROUD OF YOURSELF

Of yourself always be proud!
Whether alone or in a crowd!
Live your life with zeal and zest,
Always try to be your best!

To begin this chapter, let me share a few experiences that I had when growing up. From the time I was born I was taught that to be blind was negative and thought of as a very undesirable condition. It was not to be talked about, and I should hide the fact that I was blind as much as possible. People would not even mention the word "blind" in front of me, because it was so sad, so unfortunate. In fact, for many years of my life I did try to hide the fact that I could not see. I tried to act as if I could see. Think, please think, of how much of life I denied myself by trying to make others think I could see. As a young man, for instance, I would not consider reading a Braille book while riding on a bus-after all, that would let others on the bus know that I could not see.

When I describe my earlier years, I've used the words "taught" and the words "learned" to be ashamed of being blind." But as I matured I understand that those were only perceptions. I interpreted not being able to see in a negative manner. Unfortunately, I did not see myself in a positive fashion. Yes, I must have learned that from others, but it was my internal feelings and perceptions that led me to view myself in an unwholesome way.

For instance, I remember my mother taking me to the doctor when I was a teenager. The doctor did not know that I was blind. I heard mom quietly and secretly whisper to the doctor that I was blind. My interpretation was that to be blind was so terrible that it could not be mentioned aloud in my presence. Mom's outlook on blindness, I am sure, was because of the general public's perception of being blind. Namely, that it is not good to be blind and that the word should not even be mentioned out loud in front of a person who is blind.

Thank goodness that perspective has changed dramatically over the last 70 years. The general view of low vision and blindness has improved very much. Our culture now has a more positive and wholesome view of blindness. I am delighted with this important new perception.

I want to acknowledge that my mother was a loving and kind mom. She cared about me, and she helped me to achieve a great deal. Wonderfully, she was the person who found my teaching job back in 1956. She showed me that I was an important member of our family. The fact that, in this book, I shall mention negative things, is because I am looking at what should not have happened to me, and to encourage my readers to avoid similar experiences. In other words, don't allow yourself to be embarrassed because you are blind or have low vision. Be proud of who you are and enjoy your abilities. Do not berate yourself in any way. Focus on, develop, and enjoy all of your many attributes.

As already mentioned, I went away from home in order to go to school at age five. I attended the Michigan School for the Blind, and we lived on the campus at the school. When I was in the tenth grade, I realized that I wanted to live in the world with sighted people. So I asked the Dean of Students if I could take classes at Sexton High School in Lansing, Michigan. Sexton was several miles away from the Michigan School for the Blind. I was the first student at the Michigan School for the Blind to ask for this permission. After much discussion, permission was granted, but I had to PROMISE that I would carry a white cane as I traveled while taking two buses to Sexton High and two buses back to the school. Of course, I had to promise that I would be faithful about carrying a white cane—please enjoy my lack of sincerity!

Why did the Dean of Students make me promise to use a white cane? The reason is that I always refused to use a white cane. Why, you might ask? Because it told people that I was blind, and since I was ashamed of being blind, I wanted to keep that fact a secret. Now I do not think the Dean knew why I refused to carry a cane, but I will delve into that missing part of my education later.

Initially, a partially sighted friend, Ed Martin, rode with me back and forth on the bus to teach me the ins and outs of bus riding. My history teacher, Miss Johnson, got a call one day as I sat in class. The call told her that I would be taking the buses home, by myself, starting that day. I was sitting next to a very nice girl named Sally Cole. She leaned over and sweetly said: "I take the bus downtown every day. Let's ride together." Sally thrilled me as I thought how nice it would be to have a wonderful girl to ride with me on the bus downtown. However, I was ashamed of and felt inadequate, based on what I had learned about being blind. Right at that very moment I decided that I certainly was not going to take my cane while being with superb Sally. Unknown to me, I was being followed by Mr. Heatherington, my Gym teacher, who was also our football coach at Michigan School for the Blind.

When Sally and I got off the bus downtown, she took a bus south and I took one north. The stop before I was to get off I heard the bus bell ring, and I heard footsteps coming up the aisle. I knew those steps—they were Mr. Heatherington's. I had been followed and therefore was caught without my cane. You can imagine my fear.

When I got back to school I had to dress for football practice. To get to the field I had to walk past the coach's office, which filled me with extreme fear, especially when he called to me. He said, "Ted, you know you failed an exam today, don't you?" I simply replied, "Yes, Coach." Then much to my amazement he simply said, "See you out on the field." Bless Mr. Heatherington.

The point of this story is that I had been taught that I should not act as a person without sight. My thought was that a white cane told Sally and the world that I could not see, as if Sally didn't know that already, and that not having vision was so awful that I needed to hide it from myself and others. In truth, others certainly knew it, and I was conveying a wrong and terrible message to them about blindness. Instead, I should have conveyed to them that I was blind and that it did not matter. Doing so could have made them comfortable and at ease with my interesting characteristic of being without sight. How unfortunate for me to have held such miserable perceptions.

The truth is that I should have welcomed Sally's offer and told her that I needed to grab my cane on our way out the door to the bus. I should have been proud of the independence the cane gave me. I should have been proud of who I was and that my blindness was not important in terms of who I am. I wish I had known then that there is nothing wrong at all with being blind. Through my actions and words I could have conveyed this powerful, healthy notion to myself, to others, and especially to Sally. In short, I should have enjoyed Sally and let her enjoy me. She was my friend, and the fact that I was without vision was irrelevant to her. In fact, one time I told her that I was the president of the bachelor's club at MSB. She promptly responded, "I'm coming over there and I'm going to get you out of such a crummy club." Had I not been so fearful and lacking in confidence I am sure that Sally and I would have had a more flourishing friendship. We would have done things together during and after school. She would have been even a better friend.

I hope that I am able to convince those of you who are blind, parents of a blind child, and teachers and friends of someone who is blind or has low vision, that an individual's thoughts and feelings about being blind have a huge influence on their lives. How people feel about themselves and how they relate to others makes a difference. The dreams they have, the goals they set, the very way they conduct their life, will be seriously impacted by every thought and feeling they have about themselves.

Here is an important repeat of the first words of this chapter:

Of yourself always be proud!
Whether alone or in a crowd!
Be proud of the fact that you are blind,
Keep this thought in the front of your mind!

Chapter Summary

Be happy and delighted with who you are. Be comfortable and proud of yourself. Further, behave so that other people are comfortable being with you. Let people know that being blind is no big deal. That will help them to be totally at ease with you.

Chapter Humor

Note: The following story is not intended to be offensive. I have shared it with my fantastic wife Laura and my friend Gene. They enjoyed the humor.

In 2004, when Laura and I moved into our retirement apartment, I was walking down the hall to go to the car to get our groceries. Just before opening the outside door a lady and I happened to rub shoulders—very unobtrusively. She must have been in a bad mood for she yelled out: "Jesus Christ, are you blind?" I smiled and kindly replied, "Well lady, you're half right. I'll let you decide which half!"

CHAPTER 3

SELF-TALK

As you live and as you walk
Monitor each moment your Self-Talk

To open this most important chapter let me tell you about Self-Talk. The term is capitalized because I deem it to be important. Self-talk is the thoughts, beliefs, and statements we say to ourselves as we go through our day. We need to be aware of our thoughts. We need to monitor our thoughts. And, if and when necessary, we need to modify them in order to live at our best and be happier. My purpose in devoting a chapter of my book to Self-talk is to discuss the value and the importance of it.

I was introduced to Self-talk one Sunday when my awesome wife Laura and I were in the bookstore at The Church of Today, a Unity church in Warren, MI. Laura discovered a book titled <u>What To Say When You Talk To Yourself</u> by Shad Helmstetter, PhD. Laura and I were on an adventure to improve our lives, so we were interested in something we had never heard of. We purchased the book, and then every night as we lay in bed, Laura read a little of the book aloud. We found profound value in using Self-talk. Upon completion of the book I was so excited about it that I had it transcribed into Braille. I still have my Braille copy and would happily loan it to anyone who contacts me at tedlennox@gmail.com.

Now let's move into exploring Self-talk and the different levels of Self-talk. I am using the word "levels" because that is what Shad

Helmstetter named them. He identifies five, but for the purposes of this book, I will consider only the first four levels. First, I will offer an explanation of each level, its application to life in general, and then look at each level from the point of view of blind or visually impaired persons. Let me be very clear about my terminology. When I use the term "visually impaired" I am referring to children and adults with some vision, as well as children and adults who are totally blind.

Level One Is "I CAN'T"

A person is in Level One when he or she is saying to himself or herself. "I can't learn how to use a computer." If you think and feel this way, you either won't make the effort to learn how to become a computer user or, as you are working at learning, you will be telling yourself "I can't operate a computer" or have similar negative thoughts. Here are some likely thoughts, which limit a person who is considering learning how to use a computer:

- Computers are too difficult for me.
- I'm not smart enough to learn to use a computer.
- I don't think I will ever be good at working computers.

Here's a favorite episode to demonstrate this. It is Sunday afternoon, February 7, 2010, and I am at my daughter Amy's home. She and her husband Jesse are napping. They have a water-filtering piece of equipment that I am not familiar with. It currently needs refilling, and I am thirsty. At first my thought was "I'll have to wait because I don't know how to refill it." Then, I censored that negative thought and said to myself, "Wait just a minute! I will see what I can do. I'll bet I can fill the filter tank and get a drink." Proud, pleased, and peppy, I just disconnected the hosing after the water tank was filled. I took my cup and enjoyed the fresh water. It would not have happened had I stopped at my first thought, "I can't do this because I don't know how."

Let's view the "I Can't" level of thinking relative to being partially sighted or blind. Say your friends like to play golf and you would enjoy playing with them, but you have thoughts like this: "I can't play golf, after all—I can't see." Or, "I'd like to play golf, but since I can't see, no one would play with me." If you think these "I can't" thoughts about ANY area of your life, you won't even try. Say to yourself, "I can play golf and I would like to. I think my friends would be glad to include me and all I need to do is let them know that I want to learn and I'd like to play with them." In fact, once you make the decision to call your friend, you need to talk to yourself right at that moment and say, "I'm going to give my friend a call now". My thought is that my friend would welcome the chance to play with me and we will have a great time. I repeat the thought, "We will have a great time." By changing your thinking, you've opened the door to playing golf.

Level Two Is "I WISH I COULD". "I WOULD REALLY LIKE TO". "MAYBE SOMEDAY I WILL TRY"

An example of Level Two thinking would be a person who says, "I wish I could lose 20 pounds" or "I would like to lose 20 pounds." If that is where you stay with this thought, nothing will change, you'll just keep wishing. Now wishing is not all bad, because it might lead to something great, namely losing 20 pounds. But as long as you just wish, nothing will happen. You've got to go beyond "I can't" or "I would like to."

A blind or partially sighted person might think, "I wish I would not feel inadequate about being blind, or partially sighted." Yes, this is a great wish but you and I should not, and need not, feel inadequate. We can feel able, adequate, and achievement-bound, by moving on to Level Three.

Level Three Is "I CAN" and "I WILL"

Level Three is aimed at specific characteristics, goals, skills and attitudes. Therefore, the phrase "I can" is especially relevant. When a person is putting Level Three into practice, he or she says and thinks like this:

- "I can get good grades in school."
- "I can find a job."
- "I can handle problems constructively."

When in the "I will" mode, one would be saying or thinking,

- "I will no longer bite my fingernails."
- "I will remember to compliment my wife."
- "I will tell my father how much I appreciate him."

Now in terms of having low or no vision, take a brief look at the kind of Self-talk we may use. Again, we should continually monitor our thinking about low vision or lack of vision. We need to become very clear about our internal thoughts in this respect, as well as in other areas of our life. We need to be telling ourselves that lack of vision doesn't matter. We have many abilities and talents to develop that do not need vision. We need to use our abilities and to keep telling ourselves that we are able and capable. Keep your mind focused and your Self-talk on using and developing your skills and talents. Keep the "I can," thoughts dominant in your thinking.

Many years ago I smoked a pipe. Several times I tried to quit smoking. Had I known then about Level 3 thinking I am sure that I would have stopped smoking much sooner. When I decided to stop my tobacco habit I was at Level Two of Self-talk. What I should have done, to get on the path to quit smoking, was use one of Shad's exciting recommendations. Each time I lit my pipe I should have told myself something like this: "I no longer smoke." "I have given up smoking for good." Think of this, here I am smoking away and telling myself that I no longer smoke. What am I doing? Am I lying to myself? No. I am planting an extremely important seed into my mind. After just a few days of that kind of Self-talk I probably would have put my pipe away and continued my "I Can" Self-talk.

Level Four Is "I AM"

Level Four deals with an individual internally. That is, the way a person perceives himself or herself. It is demonstrated when one says or thinks:

- "I am a happy person."
- "I am confident."

- "I am enthusiastic about living."
- "I use positive Self-talk."

Some blind and visually impaired people have learned to think thoughts like the following:

- "I am a capable person despite my blindness."
- "I am capable even though I have low vision."

From my point of view, although there is a positive indication in those statements, they lean to the negative side. Employing Self-talk would improve the statement. A blind person could say, "I am one capable person. Blindness is just one of my characteristics. I have other characteristics such as "I'm 5'10", I'm a good singer; my hair is brown—at least that's what they tell me!"

For someone with low vision, the situation is similar. The person is thinking, "I have low vision, but I am still capable." Again, the positive indication is there, but it can be improved by saying, "I am an able and capable person. I have low vision but that's just one of my many characteristics."

A recent incident in my life is in keeping with Level Four "I AM" thinking. I was substitute teaching at Lincoln Park High School, Lincoln Park, Michigan. I was subbing for my good friend Kim, teacher of the blind and visually impaired. One of the eleventh grade students asked me how long I had been blind. I told him that I was born without sight. His immediate response was "That's so sad!" That led to a serious and significant discussion about his concept and whether it was or was not sad. I hope I led him to believe that it was not sad at all, and I made sure that my Self-talk did not think it sad.

Chapter Summary

Monitor your Self-talk. Be aware and conscious of what you are thinking and saying to yourself. Change the thoughts that are not positive.

Keep your Self-talk positive, productive, and loaded with statements of confidence!

Use "I can" and "I am" consistently.

<u>Chapter Humor</u>

A riddle: Why did the jelly roll?

****

Answer: Because it saw the apple turnover.

CHAPTER 4

MOBILITY AND ORIENTATION

An Introduction to Chapters 5, 6, and 7

In this chapter I will introduce mobility and orientation skills that I think are important for those of us who are blind or have low vision. The emphasis in the upcoming three chapters will be on confident and efficient movement. There will be a short statement about each skill. Please keep an open mind to see if what I say has meaning and value. The topics in Chapter Five are white canes, leader dogs, and GPS devices. Next we will explore the value of orientation skills mentioned in Chapter Six, including left to right, front to back, compass and map coordinates, and numbers on the clock. Chapter Seven looks into the importance of developing visualization and acoustic skills. These include creating mental pictures, tongue clicking, having steel heel plates on shoes, and counting steps.

Orientation concepts are extremely valuable when it comes to being an effective traveler. I am excited about discussing these skills with you. Mobility and orientation topics were never brought to my attention as I was growing up. Information such as this would have helped me develop my skills with much more confidence and understanding. If my teachers and parents had known, they could have introduced me to effective use of various mobility and orientation skills. Doing so would have encouraged me to use those tools.

Here are the two key concepts for freedom and orientation in the language of my poetry:

> Develop your freedom and agility,
> Be excited as you increase your mobility.

Chapter Humor

Read this one aloud. It will enhance the humor if you read it to someone.

Question: Why is 6 afraid of 7?

****

Answer: Because 7 8 9.

CHAPTER 5

MOBILITY SKILLS

Move about with confidence and joy,
This should be true for every girl and boy!

<u>Chapter Preview</u>

We will be covering three topics in this chapter—using the white cane, having a leader dog, and employing GPS devices.

THE WHITE CANE

When I was a boy, somehow I learned that carrying a white cane was a sign of being inadequate. It symbolized that you were not as capable as others. What a terrible concept for a person to have in mind. Thank the Good Lord that I have trashed this notion. My opinion is that one should be proud to carry a white cane. The freedom and confidence it provides cannot be overstated.

I want to admit that, during my four years at Michigan State University, I did not even own a white cane. I did not need to own one and even if I had, I would not have used it. Now I know how unfortunate that was. I could have used it all over campus. The reason I didn't, of course, was my notion that it conveyed a message of incompetence. I wish my teachers had helped me understand that the white cane is a tool for freedom and independence, and may even serve in developing friendships. A white cane would have told others that I am blind. It may have made them more comfortable around

17

me. I had some sensational friendships at Michigan State. I love to tell about Mac Lot, Phil Mearron, Dick Lawrence, Lloyd Spear, Vonnie Emerson, Mary Adams, Jan Berry, and Allison Stafford. My use of a white cane could have led to many more of those wholesome and marvelous relationships.

In a sense, the white cane is an extension of our sense of touch. It allows us to reach out in front of where we are to determine what is or is not there. It also gives us information about what is ahead of us in our immediate environment. The cane provides us freedom of movement and a great sense of confidence. It is a super tool for independence. I wish I had learned that years ago.

In addition, the cane protects us from potential injury. For instance, when we carry a cane while crossing a street, the driver of a car is aware of the fact that we cannot see, and hopefully that will keep him from running into us. As we walk along the sidewalk, the cane will inform a bicyclist that we cannot see them coming toward us. The white cane provides us with a lot of safety. Another benefit of carrying a white cane is being able to know what is in front of us. It also allows us to move faster and with more confidence.

There are different kinds of white canes. In general, some of them are just straight and you cannot collapse them; others are collapsible. Collapsible canes fold up and can be put in a pocket, purse or backpack. I use a collapsible cane. Again, I encourage experimenting to decide what kind of cane is preferred. Incidentally, there are also different kinds of tips for the canes.

One might raise a question as to how long the cane should be. I happen to have canes of different lengths. One is 54 inches and the other is 60 inches. I recommend that you try different length canes to see what is best for you. An individual's height might make a difference. If I were seven feet tall, I would need a longer cane than if I were five feet tall.

One more concept, a really important one, is about being comfortable. This "concept of comfortability" as I call it, makes others, as well as oneself, at ease. To a degree, if I carry my cane proudly, I am telling myself that the fact that I am blind or have low vision is just fine with me, that I am comfortable and at peace with myself. If I feel that way, then the chances are excellent that I will be putting others at ease, and they will be comfortable with me. My blindness will stimulate their interest and open acceptance of me as a whole person. That is another idea I wish I had learned when I was a boy.

LEADER DOGS

Teachers did not teach mobility to any extent when I was a boy. Reluctantly, I recall that, among my teachers and other staff members, it was conveyed to us that to have a leader dog implied that one was not quite adequate as a traveler—at least that was my interpretation as a boy. It was the feeling and perception that I picked up and integrated into my thinking. Therefore, we did not know anything about the possibility of using a leader dog for independent travel.

In my opinion, just mine, I think we should have been given some kind of introduction and instruction in the use of a leader dog. Perhaps someone from the Leader Dog School could have come to teach us about the value of a dog guide, and we could have made visits to one of the dog training schools. Moreover, it would have been ideal to be exposed to people using leader dogs. I think we actually could have had an ongoing class about mobility just as we had math class. It could have been called "The Joy and Value of Having a Leader Dog for Mobility".

In addition to the advantages a person has when traveling with a dog, there is another benefit in that the dog connects its owner with others. Many people like dogs and are attracted to them, so your leader dog can open the door to acceptance and to friendship. In fact, some of my friends who have leader dogs laughingly and joyfully tell me that people pay attention to their dog and sort of ignore them. Consider the notion of a guide dog leading to meeting new people and making new friends.

If I were to go back to teaching visually impaired and blind youngsters, I would continually weave into my teaching program some knowledge about, and experiences with, leader dogs. I would open the door of possibilities for my students with the understanding that this is an option and something for them to intelligently consider. I would include the parents of my students in developing appreciation for and understanding of the value of a guide dog. Had I been aware of it during my teaching years, I would have done much more to educate my students about independence and the various mobility options available to them. All of this could have been positive and exciting for us.

GLOBAL POSITIONING SYSTEMS

The typical and commonly accepted abbreviation for the above heading, Global Positioning Systems, is GPS. Basically, a GPS system can inform you of your whereabouts any place on earth. Further, it can aid in guiding you where you wish to go. The significance of a GPS device to blind and visually impaired individuals is the speech feature, specifically, providing directions in cars and when a person is walking.

I had fun when I bought my first GPS and loaded it into my BrailleNote. My first discovery was that I was able to help my wife Laura with her driving because she didn't have to read traffic signs or look for street signs. I was able to tell her where to turn, or when we were approaching a restaurant that we were seeking. I enjoyed that, and it allowed Laura to just drive and not need to be watching for streets signs and traffic instructions. I loved being able to say, "Laura, maybe you should slow down. You're going 72 miles per hour and the speed limit is 70." We both got many laughs as I monitored her driving. And I was able to be a back-seat driver for the first time ever!

PacMate, BrailleNote, and BrailleSense notetakers, which are discussed in Chapter 9, all have capability to load GPS software. Besides the software that can be added to the above notetakers, there are at least two other GPS systems that I am aware of. One is called

Breeze, which is a HumanWare product, and the other is called the Kapten Plus. At some point I recommend that a blind student get and learn to use one of these devices by high school age.

Dennis Opoka is one of my former elementary school students. He and I both went to Michigan State University. Dennis uses a GPS and has said that it sure would have been nice to have had a GPS when moving around campus. I echo his sentiments. I would have loved to have had my GPS when I arrived at MSU. I remember my first week getting lost and ending up in a girl's dorm!

I am pleased that mobility instructors today are teaching the use of GPS systems to high school students. Wow! Things have changed so wonderfully since I was a student.

Many thanks to all for whom I wrote this chapter. I've learned a lot about mobility, about myself, and about the advances that have been made which are benefitting today's blind and visually impaired students.

Chapter Summary

Developing mobility skills is exciting and important.

- Using a white cane has many benefits. It is a great mobility tool. Be proud of it and further your independence.
- Having a guide dog is an outstanding means to being successfully independent.
- Knowing GPS devices provides many benefits

Chapter Humor

Question: Why should you eat shoe polish and yeast before going to bed each night?

****

Answer: So that in the morning you will rise and shine!

CHAPTER 6

LEARNING ORIENTATION SKILLS

Fill your mind with confidence and thrills,
Have fun developing your orientation skills.

Chapter Preview

The focus of this chapter is to show ideas and concepts that help develop orientation skills. These skills in directional positioning include left and right, front and back, compass and map coordinates, and numbers on a clock face.

LEFT AND RIGHT, FRONT AND BACK

It is true that everybody learns left and right as they grow up but I am pointing out that, although left and right are simple and basic concepts, it is especially significant that everyone with a vision problem learns to use them. Every parent and every teacher should teach left, right, front, and back to their children and students as early as appropriate.

NORTH, SOUTH, EAST, WEST

I cannot overemphasize what a big help a compass is for someone who is blind or has low vision. If, for instance, you were coming to visit me when I lived in Wyandotte, I could give you these directions: "When you reach the corner of Fort and Vinewood, turn east and go two blocks. At 22nd Street, turn north. My house is on the southwest corner of the intersection of Vinewood and 22nd." My directions are clear and easy to understand. How wonderful it is to clearly understand and use compass directions like these. Parents, teachers, mobility instructors, all should work diligently with students to develop compass skills.

Here is a good way to teach students how the compass directions work, and how to easily remember them. It's a cute saying that says it all: "Never eat soggy waffle". Note the first letter of each word. The "N" in never, is north, the "E" in eat, is east, the "S" in soggy, is south, and the "W" in waffles, is west. So, teach and remember "Never eat soggy waffles!"

The compass can also be used to teach that a circle has 360 degrees. Start at the top of the circle, which is North. Moving one's finger and you're thinking, to the right and directly East, you have moved 90 degrees. Moving directly South, you are at 180 degrees. Continuing the circle, moving directly West, you are at 270 degrees. Then it's back to North, and you have completed 360 degrees.

I like to say:
North, South, East, or West
To know the compass is the best!

USING A FACE CLOCK TO TEACH ORIENTATION

Knowing directions is important and vital to being an effective traveler. Using an imaginary clock face is one way to teach this. It can best be taught by presenting it as a circle. It should be positioned with twelve o'clock at the top, three o'clock to the right, six o'clock at the bottom and nine o'clock at the left. When I teach you as if you are seated at a table to eat, and I tell you that your glass of water is at twelve o'clock, you'll know right where to look. This is so much more meaningful than someone setting down your water and saying, "Your water is up here". Consider hearing the word, "HERE!" such an ambiguous word. It can lead to miscommunication and perhaps spilled water.

Here is an example from my life. My wonderful wife Laura, when we were first married, would occasionally say, "Please give me that book over there." Of course I would ask her with a smile, "Where, for goodness sake, is "over there?" Then she'd correct her statement and say, "How about getting me that book on the table at nine o'clock?" I'd know right where to go to get her book. How clear, how meaningful!

Another story in terms of direction and involving the lady I love is Laura asking me to get the groceries from our car. She would not say that the car is parked "out there in the street". Rather, she'd tell me the car is on the street at eleven o'clock from the front door. I knew the exact location of the car. It made life so easy and so enjoyable.

TEACHING OTHERS TO USE DIRECTIONS TO ASSIST

I am currently living at Henry Ford Village in Dearborn, Michigan in a nice retirement community. I usually go to the dining room for dinner about 6:00. The high school and college students who escort me to a table are such fun. When I would meet one of them for the first time and we'd reach the table she would say something like this: "Your chair is right over there and behind you." In order to make them and me comfortable, I taught them to just put my hand on the back of the chair so I would know right where the chair was and where to sit. No fumbling and stumbling on my part while looking for the chair. It put me so much more at ease and it put the girls at ease knowing what to do and how to do it.

One evening at dinner my waitress was Ava. I asked her to tell me where my food was located, based on a clock face. She hesitated so I explained to her what I meant, describing the 12:00, 3:00, 6:00, and 9:00 positions. She caught on right away and told me that my fish was at 12:00, my vegetables at 2:00, and spinach at 9:00. That conversation made me aware of the changes to digital display of time on clocks. Now a clock may say 12:05 for five minutes after twelve. So the orientation skill taught using a traditional face is still powerful but at times it may need some explaining as it did with Ava. She quickly adapted and was happy to do so. In fact, she enjoyed the communication between the two of us. She said that next time she'll just tell me where my food is located using the traditional clock face.

Every once in a while in a public restaurant I'll even have an alert and knowledgeable waitress bring my plate and say, "Okay, your chicken is at twelve o'clock, potatoes are at six o'clock; peas are at nine o'clock and the muffin at three o'clock." How clear and exciting for me.

To further this notion, I am suggesting that it could be applied to a physical setting. One might describe a room in a house, in this instance a kitchen. Standing in the doorway one could say, "The sink is at two o'clock, the stove at twelve, the refrigerator at nine, and the back door at eleven." That would provide a clear picture for a blind or low vision person. Now with this example it would be more meaningful and more valuable to simply explore the kitchen and form an internal picture.

MOBILITY—ALONE OR WITH SOMEONE

Walking comfortably with others is a pleasant experience. In addition, it can contribute to one's physical fitness. There are different ways to walk with others. The person who is blind is the expert in most cases but I think about uniting people so it's important to be comfortable individually and with each other. The person with low vision or who is blind should take the lead and tell the sighted person how they would like to walk with them.

I prefer to take the arm of the sighted person just above their elbow. Thus, I am just a wee bit behind the sighted individual. If, for example, they step up a curb or go down the steps, I know it slightly ahead of time. I am warned nonverbally about curbs, steps, turns and so forth. This means that the person walking with me does not have to be as careful, although verbal cues are valuable in many cases. If you have sight, try it sometime. Put on a blindfold and go with a friend. First take their arm and go for a walk; then have them take your arm and walk. You will see how different it is and how much easier it is when you have their arm because their body communicates lots of information to you and makes moving comfortable for you both.

I know blind people who do that differently. One of my former students says he puts his hand on the person's shoulder as they walk. Then you are a bit farther behind the sighted person and that could hinder communication just a little between the two of you. Some people take their partner's arm just above the elbow like I do, but they hold it very lightly. I personally prefer to have a firm grip of my partner's arm because I believe I get better body communication.

My former student and current friend, Dennis, has told me that he can see light and dark. As he walks on the sidewalk, if there is a car parked across the sidewalk he will see the car's shadow. He says just having a little vision, in this case light and dark, can be very helpful in terms of mobility. Anyone should put to good use whatever little vision they have.

I am reiterating now what we've talked about before. Namely, be proud of who you are. Be comfortable with yourself and put others at ease with your low or lack of vision. That is, help them to be completely at ease with the status of your vision. I have known many blind children who did not know and had not been taught this outlook. This is so important. I wish someone had taught me that when I was young. In retrospect I am amazed at the things I overlooked as a teacher. If I could go back, I would teach all of these valuable and stimulating orientation skills.

Chapter Summary

Directional Positioning includes:

- Learning left and right, front and back
- Learning map and compass coordinates
- Using a clock face for directions
- Teaching others to walk with you
- Mobility techniques

Always fill your mind with confidence and thrills,
Have fun developing your orientation skills.

<u>Chapter Humor</u>

Question: What happened when a dentist married a manicurist?

****

Answer: They fought tooth and nail!!

CHAPTER 7

VISUALIZATION AND ACOUSTICS

We all need to realize
How important it is to visualize.

Chapter Preview

I am covering two critical topics in this chapter. The first will be about the value of visualizing. Then we will investigate the importance of using acoustics. Both are truly fascinating topics.

VISUALIZING

The term visualizing seems a little strange when we are discussing people who are blind or who have low vision. Maybe we should use the term "tactualizing". The word "tactualize" can be used to mean the same for a blind person, as "visualize" does for a sighted person. This is something for all of us to speculate about. I will use the term "visualize" and the term "mental picture" synonymously.

I often visualize many different items and places. I will share one of the internal pictures that I am currently enjoying, hoping it will get you personally involved in visualizing. I am lying in bed; it is 11:00 PM; and my BrailleNote is on my belly. I wonder if that is easy for you to visualize.

The scene for another example of visualization finds me physically in Florida, visiting my brother. I am visualizing the state where I live—Michigan. I am picturing the Lower Peninsula. My mind pictures exactly where some major cities and key places are located.

Right now I am picturing Traverse City, which is in the northwest corner of the state. Next, I am picturing Lansing in the middle of the state. Now I am picturing Ann Arbor. Whoops! My mind, by my choice, just traveled to the Mackinac Bridge, which connects Michigan's Upper and Lower Peninsulas. Actually, I had the joy of walking the five-plus mile bridge last Labor Day, with many others in this annual event that attracts thousands.

I want you to know how I am so able to visualize Marvelous Michigan. By pointing on my left hand, palm down, people have shown me approximately where the various cities are located in Michigan. The lower peninsula of Michigan is shaped like the back of your left hand.

Three years ago my brother Frank and I developed a booklet titled <u>Marvelous Michigan</u>. We created three tactile maps—one of the Lower Peninsula, one of the Upper Peninsula, and one showing both peninsulas. I would like to have had a tactile picture of Michigan when I was in fifth grade. I think every blind or low vision student should have tactile maps, especially of their own state. Frank and I are currently discussing such a project with a gentleman from the Florida School for the Blind. One more example of a mental picture that has meaning for me is standing just inside the entrance of my apartment. The kitchen is on the left, the bathroom on the right. Straight ahead I am picturing the living room. Walking about twelve feet toward the living room, I visualize a door on my right and a door on my left. They lead to the bedrooms.

Learning can be enhanced with "touch pictures". Ten years ago I met an inspiring lady named Katie Snyder. She and Anna Dresner and I wrote a book called A Simple Guide to Word for Kids. Katie helped me insert "touch pictures" to expand the understanding of computers. We had ten drawings. Among them are the desktop, the Microsoft Word opening screen, the spell checker screen, and the shut down screen. These pictures were designed, not from the perspective of the eye, but to be meaningful to the fingers. "Touch pictures" are much different from pictures that are to be seen with the eye. They are simpler, less detailed, and larger.

My final visualizing example comes from the fact that I like college football. Now the mental pictures I have give me a wonderful picture of the following as I enjoy the games:

- Hash marks run down each side of the length of the field.
- A football field is 100 yards long and 53-1/3 yards wide.
- Goalposts stand at each end of the field ten yards beyond the goal line.

When I was a boy I really wanted to know the exact geometric structure of the goalposts. How was I going to get such an understanding? I decided to climb the goalposts. I went up one side, sat on the crossbar, slid across it to the other end and slid down the other side. I have enjoyed my picture of the goal post structure so much for the last 65 years that recalling that wonderful experience brings me close to tears.

One day my friend John and I were teaching computer skills to two blind students, both eleven years old. I suggested to John that he provide the kids with a simple tactile picture of the screen. He correctly said to me that they did not function mentally as I do; they don't visualize the computer screen, they just go with words. Only now does it strike me that I should have been teaching the boys how to visualize.

What I'm suggesting is that visualization skills can, and should definitely, be taught. Being good at visualizing can increase one's mobility ability and enrich and improve one's learning in general. For instance, if you are given directions from point A to point B, it would help to construct an internal picture of the route, thus giving one considerable freedom and confidence. Once again, if I were 22, and understood what I understand now, I would have found ways and taken time to help and teach my students to develop their visualizing skills.

I have included three tactile pictures to illustrate and underscore how touch pictures are different from visual pictures. The three pictures show a baseball diamond, football field, and bowling lane. Please note their simplicity and spaciousness. They convey understanding for someone with little or no vision.

BaseBall

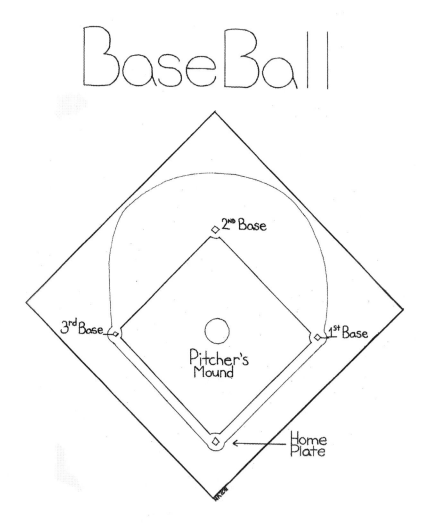

BASEBALL DIAMOND

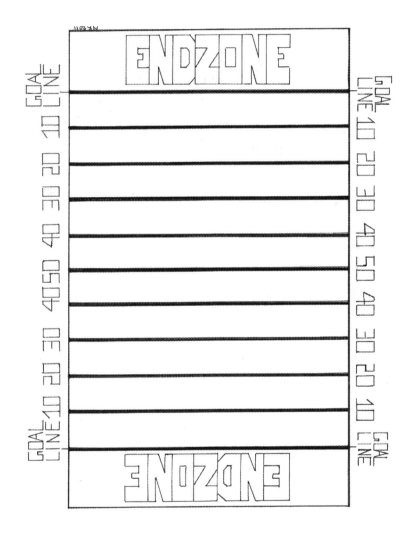

FOOTBALL FIELD

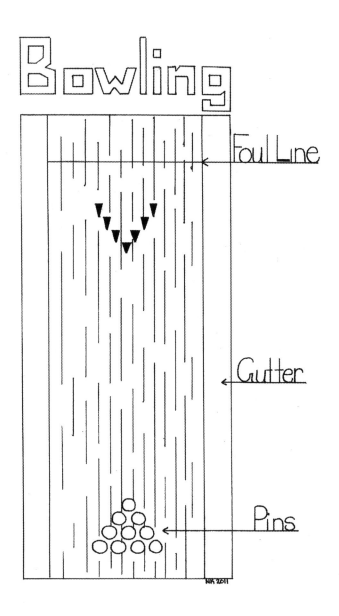

BOWLING LANE

ACOUSTICS

TONGUE CLICKING

Making clicking sounds with the tongue can provide much helpful information about the area in which one is walking because the sound goes out and then returns to your ears. With this easy method of using sound waves, you can tell if something, like a tree, is in front of you. In the apartment building where I live, unfortunately for me, the halls are all nicely carpeted. I hear very little sound as I am walking or as others are walking toward me. However, as I get close to where the hallway turns I start clicking my tongue. When I reach the turn, which is an open area, the sound waves are totally different than they are when I am walking down the hall. Using this technique makes my walking easy, efficient and comfortable.

There are two other means of sending out sound waves—snapping the fingers and using a hand-held clicker. I came across my clicker when my friend Nina and I ran a 5-kilometer race in Downtown Detroit. I highly recommend this mobility aid to everyone who is blind, and also suggest it be taught early. The idea is to learn about your environment by sending out sound waves and interpreting those waves as they bounce back to your ears. It is fun, and it helps to develop efficient mobility and orientation.

HEEL PLATES

For many years now I have used another mobility technique that enhances my life dramatically. It is helpful to me, and yet I have not met any other blind person who uses this terrific tool. I wear metal heel plates on my shoes. They send out a rather high frequency sound wave. I can detect objects in front and on either side of me. Our house in Wyandotte, Michigan was in a super neighborhood on the corner of 22nd Street and Vinewood. Right on that corner was a good—sized tree. When I got off the bus coming home from school, or when I'd come from the bank, my heel plates would send out sound waves. When I got within about six feet of the tree, I knew exactly when to make that turn. Likewise, when I hiked anywhere along a sidewalk, I knew if someone had parked a car across the sidewalk because I'd hear the car as a result of my heel plates sending out sound waves.

About three years ago I bought a new pair of shoes. I took them to the shoe repair shop and had heel plates put on. However, unknown to me, there was a different repairman, and he put on plastic heel plates. The plastic did not send out good, clear, sharp, sound waves. I had to go back and ask him to put the old-time metal heel plates on my shoes, and then I was in good shape again. (I recall that he and I split the cost.)

COUNTING STEPS

For years people *accused* me of finding my way by counting steps. My use of the word *accuse* is deliberate because for 70 years I refused to count steps. That attitude went back to my past where I believed that that's what they thought I did because that's what was expected of a blind person. I simply had turned away from being treated or thought of as a blind person. It's similar to me telling myself not to get my cane when Sally, from Sexton High School, said we could ride the bus together. Now I count my steps with pleasure and joy, and a powerful sense of control.

My apartment is on the fourth floor in the building where I live. Sometimes I use the stairs, and then head down the hall. There are three fans on the hallway ceiling. After going under the third fan, I count 16 steps and I am smack dab at my apartment door on the left. There are few places where I step count; in fact, I have only three other places. I am doubtful that I would ever have any locations where I'd count more than twenty or thirty steps. However, doing so is very helpful depending upon the circumstances.

Whenever I use the elevator, I enjoy a fond memory about my wife. Every once in a while when we'd ride the elevator together I'd stand with my back in front of the control panel and secretly reach behind and punch the third floor button. The elevator would stop at the 3rd floor and I'd get off with Laura. About half way down the hall she'd stop and say: "Ted! We're on the wrong floor." Then she'd realize that I had done it purposely. I enjoyed that so much.

Chapter Summary

In this chapter we have talked about the value of visualization or mental picturing for mobility. I discussed using acoustics and identified the specifics of sending out sound waves via tongue clicking and heel plates. Counting steps was presented as a good tool for locating places.

Chapter Humor

Brain Teaser: Find the names of two countries in the following sentence, using the letters in the same consecutive order as they appear in the sentence-

Engaging in plain dialog is less painful than fighting.

****

Answer: India and Spain

Postscript: Spellchecker detects that "tactualizing" is not a word. Well, it is now!!

CHAPTER 8

READING

Braille is Beautiful

I go through my day from dot to dot,
Braille is beautiful; I like it a lot,
These six little bumps have great appeal,
With my fingers I just have to feel,
The world comes alive and the world is real!

Chapter Preview

Our priority should be to teach children how to read, how to remember, and how to think. Of course this practice holds true for reading with the fingers, eyes, or ears. There are two major topics in this chapter—reading Braille and reading print. Both are critical in terms of success in school and life in general. Reading through listening is also noted.

READING BRAILLE

First and foremost, I want to make a positive statement: Braille is beautiful and Braille is fun! Parents, preschool and early elementary school teachers need to stimulate students to read. First and foremost, parents should read to children and then talk about what they are reading. If the child is blind, they should take time to show them objects and provide considerable tactile experiences. The teaching individuals need to have tools for making tactile drawings, so when they cannot show their youngster the real object, they can make simple and meaningful tactile drawings. Tools are available from the American Printing House for the Blind.

In the case of a youngster with low vision, parents should read to him or her and patiently show them pictures in the books. I am making a fervent recommendation that parents of low vision and blind children learn the basics of Braille. Not only learn it, but also enjoy Braille and show enthusiasm for it to their child. It would have been wonderful had my parents been able to learn and use Braille with me, but when I was a boy there really was no way they could have learned Braille. Now there are many easy ways.

I am recommending that parents learn at least Grade One Braille and also basic punctuation and numbers. Basic punctuation refers to the capital sign, period, and comma. I'd further recommend, especially for those who get enthused about Braille, learning what each letter in the alphabet stands for. Here are just a few examples to give you some understanding. The letter "b" by itself with a space on either side stands for the word "but". The letter "c" stands for "can"; "d" stands for "do"; and "e" for "every". The Braille contractions not only save space and paper, but also speed up reading.

As a youngster proceeds in school he or she should be reading in a definite teaching environment at least 40 minutes per day. The reading should not be incidental; it should be instructional, with emphasis on the Braille code and comprehension. The youngster should also have reading assignments to do at home. That reading is best when coordinated with the school.

I highly recommend that all youngsters who are blind or legally blind should be registered with The National Library Service for the Blind. Once registered, you can get books, magazines, and Braille music materials. The library has books available in Braille, large print, and audio format. To register, call the library and you will be guided through the registration process. You will need to establish proof that the child or adult is qualified for their services.

Children, who have some vision, but not enough to allow reading at a normal rate, should learn to read both Braille and print. One marvelous outcome that I had with many of my students was that they learned to read both print and Braille. Because they had low vision they could only read 50-60 words per minute using print, but under certain circumstances that was very helpful. They also learned to read Braille, and because they could read Braille far more rapidly, they used Braille for school and leisure reading. Many of my low vision students have told me how valuable it has been to be able to read both.

Braille proved to be fun for my daughter Marla when she was ten years old and for Amy when she was seven. For a six-week period during the summer, we had a "Banana Split" class. My two girls and four of their friends met with me on our back porch once a week. The purpose was to teach them Braille. I gave them a lesson, and then homework to write with their slate and stylus. Those who came for each class and turned in their homework each week earned a banana split at the end of the course. Happily, I took six youngsters out for banana splits in August.

Eight years later Marla, now 18 years old, had an interesting use for Braille. My wife Laura and I took Marla to Michigan State University where she was starting college. As we were unpacking I heard Marla drop a slate into her dresser drawer. I asked her why in Heaven's name she brought her slate and stylus. She quietly marched me out into the hall and whispered, "Dad, if I need some extra money I'll write to you in Braille." She continued whispering, "I have a better chance of getting some money from you than from Mom." Laura and I laughed about that many times.

FINGER READING

I want to describe how to read with the fingers by telling you how I read. I read with both hands—though I have heard of people who read with more than their index fingers. I begin with my index fingers side by side at the top of the page on the left side until I'm about half way across the top line. At that point my left index finger abandons my right index finger. The right index finger completes reading the line, as the left index finger goes back to the beginning of line one and drops down to line two to start reading across line two. About half way across line two, my right index finger meets my left index finger. My right index finger then takes over and finishes line two, while my left finger goes back to start reading line three.

One of my students named Craig came to our school from Missouri when he was in the fourth grade. Craig was a great student and a good Braille reader. He read with just one hand and with one index finger if I recall correctly. I showed Craig how my other students were reading with both hands but he was not at all motivated to make the adjustment. After a reasonable period I decided that his method worked for him and that I was doing him no service trying to change his reading style. That was in 1964. I talked to Craig a couple months ago and interestingly, he said he still reads rapidly with one hand.

READING THROUGH LISTENING

Books on tape and disks are available from libraries for the blind and physically handicapped. Again I encourage parents and teachers to have their youngsters registered with the Library for the Blind and spend time using the digital readers, thereby teaching reading by listening. This would not be too challenging, especially if you've already been reading aloud to your child.

For many years when I was teaching, I'd start the day by doing some reading to my students. Some of the books we read were Super Fudge, Freckle Juice, and The Boxcar Children. The students and I all enjoyed this start of our day. I wish there had been more to this than just reading. We could have discussed what we were reading and talked about words they didn't know. Then, at the end of the reading, we could have summarized what we had read. Some days we'd start the day with a little poetry. That, too, was rich.

Chapter Summary

It is my hope that I have conveyed the importance of reading Braille for a blind person, and the importance of learning to read both Braille and print for someone with minimal vision. All parents and teachers should be involved in encouraging and supporting reading, and ideally they should know and enjoy basic Braille.

These are my recommendations about children learning to read:

- Start reading to children early. Help them to learn, that is to see, with their fingers, or see through touch.
- Teach both print and Braille to children who have some vision.
- Parents and teachers should learn and use basic Braille. Perhaps the student's brothers and sisters might also.
- Braille reading might be taught by using two index fingers.
- Auditory reading should be taught.
- Reading needs to be fun, exciting, and interesting.

Chapter Humor

Brain Teaser: Move through the alphabet from a-z without stopping. Which three words can you find intact? The letters of each word should be in alphabetical order.

****

Answer: a, hi, no.

CHAPTER 9

WRITING

Writing is an important skill,
Whether you're Bonnie or whether you're Bill.

<u>Chapter Preview</u>

The aim of this chapter is to talk about various ways of writing. These topics will be discussed: proper fingering when writing on the Braille writer or a computer notetaker that uses six keys to write Braille, teaching correct fingering on the standard computer keyboard, and writing with a pen to sign your name. A description and the use of a slate and stylus are included. To conclude this chapter I explore the use of orientation dots on a Qwerty keyboard.

USING A PERKINS STYLE KEYBOARD

In this section of the chapter we are talking about efficiently using your fingers to write documents on a Perkins Style Keyboard. This includes the Braillewriter and the Braille Note, Pac Mate, and Braille Sense. When using this style keyboard the left index finger should press dot 1; the left middle finger should do dot 2, and the left ring finger should press dot 3. The right hand should do the same for dots 4, 5, and 6. In general the <u>space bar</u> should be pressed either with a thumb or with one of the index fingers.

If you are using the Braille Note, PacMate, or Braille Sense, it is good, very good, to use your little fingers like this-The left little finger can strike the <u>backspace</u> key, and the right little finger the <u>enter</u> key.

Now we move to the use of the thumbs. The <u>thumb keys</u> are right at the front of the Braille Note. When one's fingers are reading the braille display, the thumbs are right at the front of the Braille Note. There are four <u>thumb keys</u> separated by a bar, with two keys to the left and two to the right.

When reading using the Braille display, the <u>thumb keys</u> control how one reads. The key on the left (the previous <u>thumb key</u>) moves you back to the previous braille segment, the second key from the left (the <u>back key</u>) moves the braille display back one word.

Moving our focus to the right <u>thumb keys</u> and continuing from left to right, the third key is controlled with the right thumb. When the third key is pushed, the Braille Note moves ahead one word at a time; the fourth key jumps ahead one segment at a time. <u>Thumb keys</u> are wonderful to use when a person is reading Braille. I taught my students about the <u>thumb keys</u> (PBAN) by having them think of peanut butter and jelly, but the best I could do was "Peanut Butter And Nelly". They never had trouble keeping track of the keys from left to right. The keys are the <u>previous</u>, <u>back</u>, <u>advance</u>, and <u>next</u>. There will be more on this in <u>Chapter 11</u> when I discuss Braille notetakers.

USING A QWERTY KEYBOARD

This section deals with desktop and lap top computers, which use the QWERTY type keyboard. The letters of the word are the names of the five keys starting on the left of the top row of letters on the keyboard. I find the word fascinating. Even more interesting, as far as I know, Qwerty is the only word in English where the letter "q" is not followed by the letter "u".

Good fingering and proper teaching of it will, in most cases, help an individual to be efficient when using the QWERTY keyboard.

In 2003 I had a great student named Ernie who had a condition that prevented him from using his fingers in the normal way. Judy Phelps, a computer specialist from our Wayne County Resource Center, and I decided to teach Ernie where all the letters are on the keyboard to help him develop his own unique keyboard skills. We considered not teaching Ernie to use the computer, but with Judy's assistance, what happened is wonderful! Ernie became very competent in using the keyboard in his own special way. Further, Ernie continued to be an outstanding computer user, and is now in college studying computer technology.

My position on the importance of good typing skills is influenced by my own experience as a student. When I was in the fourth grade we were taught typing. Our teacher did not instruct, encourage, or help us to use proper fingering. In my young mind I thought it did not matter—after all, I got an "A" in the class. Consequently I did not bother to attempt to become a good typist. Then, in the eleventh grade, I turned in a paper for my English class. The teacher, Mr. Haslett, nicely, but sternly, told me how really bad my typing was. I'd made so many typing errors! To this day I appreciate his feedback.

There are many good software programs available for teaching keyboarding skills. One that I am aware of, and have used extensively with my students, is the Talking Typer program from the American Printing House for the Blind. There are others as well.

WRITING WITH PEN OR PENCIL

When I was in the fourth grade, on rare occasions I would come home from the Michigan School for the Blind. My brothers, Frank and Cecil, were both in the third grade. I would go to school with them and they would teach me to write with a pencil. I learned the capital letters but not the small case letters. I have always been grateful to them for teaching me to write the letters. I use them quite often to mark the front of an envelope, sign greeting cards, autograph the book I authored, or just for fun. They also have significance for me when I read embossed signs on restroom doors, elevator panels or drinking fountains.

Surprisingly, and I must say sadly, not once during my years at the Michigan School for the Blind were any of the students taught how to write their names. To this day, I am surprised that that was not part of the curriculum. It should be part of the schooling for every blind child. There are tactile letters available as aids to teach handwriting to children who cannot see. I highly recommend that teachers and parents get these materials and ensure that their children learn to write their names.

There are writing guides available that can be placed on a page to keep the letters in a line. I never used such a guide because I was not taught to write with a pen. Therefore, I never learned to write my name in script. I needed that skill when I graduated from high school. Fortunately, during college I met Allison, a girl from Minnesota. She was one of several people who read to me. She was a big help and became a good friend. At some point she expressed shock that I had never learned to write my name. She told me that it was essential. One day she came with pen and paper in hand, and I began to write my name. Many, many thanks to you, Allison!

SLATE AND STYLUS

The Slate and Stylus go far back in history. They were used as the only method for Braille writing for years. Although used less frequently now, they can still be purchased at the American Printing House for the Blind. Several kinds of slates and styluses for writing Braille are available. They are inexpensive as compared to a Braillewriter. The Janus type, for example, is $5.00. The website is www.shop.aph.org.

Slate and stylus, as used in this chapter, are tools for writing Braille. The **slate opens up** and a piece of paper is inserted. The stylus is hand held by the wooden top; the other end has a sharp point, like a nail, which punches dots when pressed onto the paper in the slate. There are six places to punch Braille dots—one through six—to create letters, numbers and punctuation.

I use my Braillewriter frequently. I also use my BrailleNote extensively, including, for example, writing this book. However, I still have slates and styluses, and I find them very useful. A slate and stylus are easy to carry in a pocket or purse, so I have mine with me most of the time. I like just pulling it out of my pocket and writing whenever I wish, right on the spot. In fact, when I play Scrabble with three friends, I am the scorekeeper and I use my slate and stylus at that time.

I would recommend that teachers, or others, take time to teach the use of slate and stylus and let the students decide for themselves whether it has a place in their life.

A family member, perhaps a sibling or friend, who doesn't know Braille or does not have access to a Braille writer, may want to learn to use a slate and stylus for an occasional contact with the blind or low vision person. All they need to know are the basics of Braille and be willing to practice writing from right to left. Why write from right to left? Because the dots are written face down on the paper and the paper gets turned over to read it. The technique is not difficult and lets the user write notes to their student, and do other fun things like marking their game boxes.

ORIENTATION DOTS

Some teachers and parents have applied orientation dots on letters and numbers on the QWERTY keyboard. I use them on mine. I personally have them on only five keys.—the letters f and j, and the numbers 1, 5, and 0. If I were still teaching daily, I'd experiment with how many dots are helpful for a beginner. One would need to be careful not to overdo and put too many orientation dots on the keyboard. Perhaps for a beginner one might also put such a dot on the enter key, and the backspace key. I get my orientation dots from Exceptional Teaching Aids. I find they work very well.

Now here comes an opinion. I have noted some teachers putting braille letters on all the alphabet keys. I am just wondering, and I speak with no experience, if all those braille dots get in the way. That's just a question for you, the reader, to contemplate. When I taught beginning typing skills, I used orientation dots, and I found them very helpful for my students. My recommendation is to put them on at least the f, j, <u>enter</u>, 1, 5, 0, and the <u>backspace</u> keys.

Chapter Summary

- Writing Braille using a Perkins style keyboard with emphasis on correct fingering
- Writing using Qwerty keyboards and emphasizing correct fingering
- Using pen and pencil, especially to write one's name.
- Learning the slate and stylus as a useful tool for Braille writing.
- Orientation dots are helpful.

Chapter Humor:

Brain Teaser: The word "STARTLING" has nine letters. Begin by writing the word "startling". Remove one letter at a time and make a new word each time. The last word will be one letter. You will have a total of nine words.

****

Answer: startling, starting, staring, string, sting, sing, sin, in, I.

CHAPTER 10

SCREEN READERS AND SCREEN MAGNIFIERS

Computers have opened the world to so many!
It matters not whether you're chubby or skinny!
It matters not whether you're blind or have vision!
To learn to use them is a powerful decision!

<u>Chapter Preview</u>

My purpose in this chapter is to introduce you to screen readers and screen magnifiers and their functions. I have a personal experience to tell about my introduction to a screen reader, and I will offer details for learning more about the products I present.

My first personal story has to do with the JAWS Screen Reader. In the late 1980's, my wife Laura and I were interested in computers, and I discovered that I could have a 4-month trial version of JAWS. It was named after a very popular movie titled JAWS, which you probably know about. I found it interesting that the letters j-a-w-s is the acronym for Job Access with Speech. JAWS are no longer available as a 4-month trial. Now a trial program plays for 40 minutes. When the program is nearing the end, a "message alert" tells you there are three minutes remaining, after which the user can reset the program for another 40 minutes. This unlimited access allows plenty of time to get to know JAWS.

I started my 4-month trial early in January. On April 28, JAWS told me automatically that my trial version would expire in three days. When I heard that, I popped out of my chair upstairs in our computer room and raced downstairs where Laura was reading the newspaper. I told her how much JAWS meant to me and that I'd like to buy my own copy. She immediately encouraged me to do so, and the next day I ordered my first screen reader.

SCREEN READERS

A screen reader is quite simple to understand. It speaks the text that is printed on the computer screen. For instance, if you are using Microsoft Word to write a letter, the computer will speak every word or character you write, depending on how you set it. I like to think of the example of you having written a letter to The President of the United States, and then you're being able to listen to everything you wrote. Excitedly, you can listen by line, by sentence, by paragraph, and with one simple command, you can also listen to your whole letter.

There are five different screen readers that might be of interest to you. Reading about them may be for you, like what going to an ice cream store is for me. Often there are as many as 35 flavors. I feel impatient having someone read all the choices; it's almost too much for me. I hope that the number of screen readers and the details I have listed do not overwhelm you. The websites can help you find additional information.

1. JAWS—Job Access With Speech is produced by Freedom Scientific, located in St. Petersburg, Florida. Freedom Scientific will provide a demonstration copy, which runs 40 minutes and warns you when the time is almost up. The website is www.freedomscientific.com the phone number: 800-444-4443

2. SYSTEM ACCESS is produced by the Serotek Company. My experience with it makes me recommend it as a good, and useful, screen reader. The website is www.serotek.com

3. NVDA—Nonvisual Desktop Accesibility. NVDA is a free screen reader. The company is headquartered in Australia. The home page has a very clear and understandable introduction as to what it does. It is so clear and easy to use that it could be a model for other sites. The website is www.nvda.org

4. Voiceover is produced by Apple Inc. The i-Pad, i-Phone, and i-Pod, as well as the Mac, all include speech and screen magnification. My experience has been that Apple, Inc. is unique in that the employees at their retail stores have basic training in terms of Voiceover and screen magnification and are very helpful. The website, www.apple.com/accessibility, gives clear and valuable information.

5. Windows-Eyes are produced by GW Micro. Windows-Eyes have been on the market for many years and are another highly respected screen-reading program. The home page is written in easily understood language, has a good introduction, and provides a basic understanding of the program. Go to the Windows Eyes link. The website is www.gwmicro.com

SCREEN MAGNIFICATION PROGRAMS

A screen-magnifying program will enlarge what appears on the screen, permitting a person with low vision to be able to read what's displayed. In the programs I mention, the size of the print can be controlled. The individual can determine how large the print should be and can set the screen color and screen contrast to effectively make use of his or her particular visual situation.

Here are four screen magnification programs: MAG-IC, ZoomText, and the one with Apple computer's Voiceover, and System Access.

1. Freedom Scientific produces MAG-IC. The letters MAG in the name come from Magnification; the letters IC are for In Color. MAG-IC allows a person to enlarge the screen from 2 times up to 36 times the regular size. Moreover, there are two versions of MAG-IC. One version enlarges what is displayed

on the screen. The other includes speech. The result is that you can see an enlargement of the information and also hear it spoken. The website is www.freedomscientific.com Follow the link "products", then go to MAG-IC Screen Reader. As with JAWS, Freedom Scientific provides a trial version that runs for 40 minutes—plenty of time to become comfortable with the product. You may also call Freedom Scientific at 1-800 444-4443.

2. Zoom Text is produced by aisquare. It will enlarge or magnify the screen up to 36 time's normal size. It, too, has two versions available. One magnifies what's on the screen; the other version has speech and screen magnification. The trial version gives some good experience because it lasts 60 days. One added feature is that a person can have it on a thumb drive and carry it with them. The phone number is 1-800 770-8474. The web address is www.ai-square.com.

3. Apple Computers come with a screen magnification program as part of the system.

- The Apple desktop computer called the Macintosh.
- Their iPADS
- Their iPODS and
- Their iPHONES.

One can go to any Apple store and get basic instructions on any of their products because the personnel are trained to provide assistance with the accessible programs.

4. System Access is produced by Serotek Corporation. It has both speech and screen magnification. There is a one-week trial version. The website is www.serotek.com

Feel free to contact me for additional information. My phone number is 313 846-0318. My e-mail address is tedlennox@gmail. com. When sending a message to my e-mail address, please use the following in the Subject line: "Response to your book."

Chapter Summary

This chapter offers an introduction to five screen readers and four screen magnification products.

Chapter Humor

Question: What do ducks put in their soup?

****

Answer: Quackers!!

Question: What do you call a crate of ducks?

****

Answer: A box of quackers!!

CHAPTER 11

BRAILLE NOTETAKERS

<u>Chapter Preview</u>

This chapter will cover three notetakers: BrailleNote, PacMate Omni, and Braille Sense Plus, and my explanations of what these wonderful notetakers can do. They are fabulous technology tools that can immensely enhance the lives of blind and visually impaired people. In general, all of them have the same basic functions, but they do them in different ways to a degree. I wonder how I managed to live effectively without my Braille notetaker. In fact, my notetaker is so important to me that I wrote a poem about it which tells about how sensational a notetaker is, and on a personal note, the last stanza gives me a place to express myself about my outstanding wife of forty-five and a half years.

BRAILLE NOTETAKERS

I love my Braille Note,
Upon it I dote,
It has my vote,
It's better than a car, better than a boat!

What does it do you may ask,
It will help with many a task.
It's a computer and it does so much,
It speaks to the ear and it speaks to the touch!

It will output information straight in Braille,
With my fingers I read without fail.
It also will speak to me I do declare,
Sound waves come to me right through the air!

Speech or Braille I may choose,
There's no way that I can lose.
But listen to this I want you to know,
Braille and speech together can flow!

So I can use speech or I can use Braille,
But both together can be used without fail,
Braille or speech, speech or Braille,
Or use them together, how can I fail?

I can write a note, document, or letter,
How could my life be any better?
To the Internet I can meander,
I can go to any web site and I can gander!

I can Google to my heart's content,
There's no website to which I cannot went.
A Google map I can get in Braille,
When Laura and I travel and we do not fail!

This book is written on my computer in Braille please note!
The spelling checker I used as I wrote.
The dictionary I use continually,
My vocabulary has improved fabulously!

These note takers also have a calculator,
For doing figures what could be greater?
From simple to complex you are free,
You can even deal with a little geometry.

E-mail you can send, receive, and save,
About the e-mail program I really do rave.

For the first time in my life I can read my own mail,
It's available in speech or in Braille.

There are many other things that I do,
Perhaps I might mention just a few.
There are games and music I do declare,
I just download them right through the air!

There is a program that allows you to plan,
It's great for any lady or man.
My dates and alarms it will keep,
Keeping me on schedule or wake me from sleep!

About my BrailleNote I really do rave,
I think I'll take it with me to the grave.
It helps me to live a wonderful life,
There's only one thing better and that's my WIFE!

PAC MATE OMNI

Freedom Scientific produces the PAC Mate Omni. Several models are available. Two models have only speech as their output. One model uses a Perkins style keyboard and the other uses a Qwerty style keyboard. There is an option to have either "20 cell" or "40 cell" Braille display. The website is freedomscientific.com. Click on Products and then PAC Mate Omni, or call 800-444-4443.

BRAILLE SENSE PLUS

The Braille Sense Plus is another powerful and easy to use notetaker. It has both speech and Braille output. There is a choice of a Perkins or Qwerty keyboard. The difference between these two is that the Perkins is composed of six keys that represent the six Braille dots, and an <u>enter</u> key, <u>backspace</u> key, and <u>spacebar</u>. Qwerty keyboard simply means a standard computer keyboard.

All three Notetakers that I am discussing in this chapter have Perkins Style keyboard and the option for an "18 cell" or "32 cell" display. More information about Braille Sense Plus is available at the following website: www.hims-inc.com. You can click on Products, then on Braille Sense Notetakers. You can also call them at 888-520-4467.

BrailleNote was introduced in 2000 and has continually improved since then. Like Pac Mate and Braille Sense, it is an outstanding piece of computer equipment. It writes documents, performs spell checks, sends and receives e-mail, and allows you to surf the Internet. The cell display option is "18 cell" or "32 cell".

The HumanWare Company produces BrailleNote. The website is www.humanware.com. Click the link Blindness, then go to BrailleNote. You can also call 800 722-3393. My experience is that the customer service people are easy to talk to and very helpful.

INFORMATION ABOUT CONTEXT SENSITIVE HELP

All three of the notetakers I have discussed have Context Sensitive Help. I consider it a powerful aid, especially when one is just learning to use a notetaker. It is a means for a user to get guidance and instructions about the subject they are engaged in at the moment. For example, if you have written a document and are in spellchecker but are not sure what the various commands are, all you need to do is to give the Context Sensitive Help command and you will be told how to go about spellchecking.

Technology support is extremely valuable. Tech support personnel often solve problems immediately, and my experience is that if they cannot; they investigate your problem and get back to you. All three of these companies have outstanding technology support. You can reach them by calling or writing their tech support group.

Familiarity is the key to choosing a notetaker. I find that users of notetakers recommend the kind of equipment they are using. For instance, I have had the joy of using my BrailleNote since 2002 and I think it is the greatest. I have a friend who owns a Braille Sense. He will tell you that it is the best of the three notetakers. One of my students uses the Pac Mate, and she swears by it. My point is that the piece of equipment we get to know and use is the one we think is best.

Again, as in <u>Chapter 10</u>, feel free to contact me for additional information. My phone number is 313-846-0318. My e-mail address is: tedlennox@gmail.com. When sending a message to my e-mail address, please type in the subject line: "Response to Chapter __"

<u>Chapter Summary</u>

Basic information and personal experience was shared about three notetakers:

- The BrailleNote from HumanWare
- The BrailleSense from the Hims Company
- The Pac Mate Omni from Freedom Scientific.

<u>Chapter Humor</u>

Brain Teaser: What one word can be added to "sauce," "pine" and "crab" to create a new compound word?

****

Answer: apple: applesauce, pineapple, and crabapple.

CHAPTER 12

POWER-BOOSTING THOUGHTS AND SUGGESTIONS

REALITY
Viola Lucaweicki

My thoughts are very potent things,
They hem me in or give me wings.
My thoughts create, enslave, or free,
Enrich or impoverish me!

My own thoughts make me glad or sad,
They choose decide for good or bad.
What're they be is true for me,
My thoughts are my reality!

This poem, written by a lady named Viola Lucaweicki, is one of my all-time favorites. It appears as the second poem in my book <u>DIE DAILY</u>, but I consider it a significant opener to this chapter.

<u>Chapter Preview</u>

This chapter is a collection of ideas, thoughts, opinions, and suggestions aimed at boosting one's happiness, effectiveness, joy, and confidence. You certainly may not agree with some of what I suggest, so I encourage you to think for yourself. This chapter will be broken into many headings, so I can cover a conglomeration of what I hope will be fascinating and thought-provoking subjects for your thinking.

I SEE WITH MY FINGERS

When I was a boy, no one helped me to understand the wonderful way of getting to know my world through "seeing with my fingers". No teacher, no adult, no friend ever made me realize that my fingers were my way of learning and understanding. I am quite sure that was because they functioned with their eyes, their fingers were incidental. Therefore, others did not understand the absolute importance of learning by touch. Metaphorically, my fingers are my eyes. This is an important notion. As a boy, many sighted people—especially my teachers—discouraged exploration with the fingers. If we went on a field trip, they would describe things, but discouraged touching. I remember being criticized occasionally for touching things. I was told, "You probably should not touch." Now I know that I should have been encouraged to touch and explore. Let me site two examples.

In high school we had a history class dealing with the United States. We were never exposed to a tactile map of our country, and so none us neither knew east, west, north, and south, nor did we ever have a tactile map showing the Atlantic and Pacific Oceans, Canada, and Mexico. The same was true for our state—Michigan. No map was ever provided to allow us to feel the locations of the major cities and the Great Lakes or know what both peninsulas look like.

Next is an example from my days at Michigan State College, now Michigan State University. When I took chemistry, I worked with a fellow student in the chem lab. We did experiments by measuring, heating, and mixing chemicals. I should have been doing all of those things with my hands. First, I had been taught to keep my hands mostly off. Second, the instructor did not comprehend, nor did I, how vital it was for me to be doing all those things myself. He and I both should have insisted that I do the experimenting and testing myself.

Now here's the wonderful part of this episode. As I have learned to be comfortable with myself and with my blindness, I have discovered that that also makes others comfortable. They are in a position to understand how I experience life. They encourage and facilitate my "seeing with my fingers." I can tell you how sensational it is to be comfortable and make others at ease. They accept me as I am; I accept them for who they are. What a great way to live! Here are two positive examples:

I was visiting my brother's family just outside of Chicago. I went with Josh, my nephew, to an outdoor concert on a beautiful Saturday evening. Josh's wife Mary was playing clarinet in the orchestra. Before the concert Josh and I went through a park where he showed me, among other things, army tanks and various kinds of cannons. With great interest I examined them with my fingers. Then, before the concert, we went on the stage and examined the various sections where the musicians would be sitting and where the conductor would be standing. He even showed me exactly where Mary would be sitting. I cannot tell you how much that enriched the concert for me. I was thrilled to have in my mind a picture of what everyone else was seeing.

Another illustration is about when my daughter Amy and I took her three little children to a children's farm. The finale of the visit was when the farmer allowed each student to milk the cow. After the kids were done milking Amy took me to the cow and the farmer showed me the cow's four teats. Of course, I did some milking. It was a great hands-on experience all day for the kids and for me.

The following poem serves as my conclusion to this topic. "I See with My Fingers" is in Chapter 11 of my book DIE DAILY. My friend Jan at Michigan State planted a seed about the importance of touch. At the time I didn't understand totally what Jan was saying, but as it became more meaningful, it leads to this poem.

I SEE WITH MY FINGERS

I once had a super good friend,
Her name was Jan, but I called her Toot,

She stimulated my thinking, what an awesome trend,
The thinking she inspired bore lots of fruit.
In college I was exploring items in her dormitory room,
We were talking and laughing; there was not any gloom.
A friend, whose name was Jane, was present,
Jane was lively and always so pleasant,

At a point Jane expressed in a joyful tone,
Ted's fingers are busy; he leaves nothing alone,
Toot replied, and she did not linger,
That's because Ted sees with his finger!

In many respects my fingers are my eyes,
Touching things, to understanding gives rise!
I love my fingers, I love my hand,
They add meaning to life and that is grand,

I see with my fingers night and day,
Toot brought that to my attention in a positive way!
If you are blind, then your fingers are your eyes,
She upped my awareness,
It was a wonderful surprise!

DEEP BREATHING

I include this topic because I think it is a skill, which everyone should be aware of, and practice. This topic, like several others in this book, is about things I wish I had been taught when I was a youngster. How much happier and fulfilled I would have been!

Deep breathing is helpful because it is relaxing and allows a person to be calm and to think clearly. It is one technique that removes stress and frustration. So, to clear your mind and live effectively you might want to try deep breathing.

I personally employ deep breathing often. Let's say I am maneuvering my way through a crowded room where there is lots of noise. I used to get stressed, fearing I would bump into people or embarrass myself by tripping on furniture. Now I take over my *mind* and I start to breathe deeply.

How and why do I do deep breathing?

- I zero in on the fact that I am fearful, worried, stressed, or feeling inadequate.
- I consciously take over my mind and my thinking.
- I begin the deep breathing by inhaling slowly through my nose (One can breathe more deeply through the nose than the mouth.) I feel the air expanding my diaphragm.
- I exhale slowly and completely. Doing it slowly is important because it gets the maximum amount of oxygen into your system while clearing the maximum amount of carbon dioxide out of your system.
- I start the process again.

Whenever I feel tense, I consciously put to use this type of breathing. It has made such a difference in my life. In my opinion, every child should learn and practice this powerful skill. I am committed to teaching the technique to students in my seminars and to my outstanding Grandchildren.

DEEP BREATHING

There are many ways we can breathe,
The way we do it can help us to achieve!
Tell me how I may ask,
Do I need a hose or a mask?

Deep breathing will keep your mind so clear,
It will help us live with confidence and not with fear.
Breathe through your nose and be sure to inhale,
It will help you succeed and not to fail!

Whenever you find yourself fighting stress,
Relax breath deep and do not press.

Breathing through your nose is the proper door,
Breathing through your mouth please, please ignore.

Be sure to inhale oh so deep,
An erect posture please, please keep!
Breathe in and expand your diaphragm,
And into life you'll want to scram!
Breath deep and your diaphragm expand,
Of your breathing this you should demand!

Let's pull this together and thus conclude,
Stand tall and hold your head erect,
Through your nose inhale and improve your mood!
You will notice a wonderful effect!

SITUATIONAL SELF-TALK

This section of the chapter is an extension of the discussion about Self-talk in Chapter 3 of Shad Helmstetter's book What To Say When You Talk To Your Self. The main idea here is that it is wise to use Situational Self-talk as we go from activity to activity throughout our day. It involves determining what we say to ourselves in relation to what we are presently doing. In other words, we should be aware of our internal conversation. However, awareness is not enough. We should control, guide, and direct what we say to ourselves. Here are some examples that I have used.

I have been in an audience listening to a speaker present an important topic. At the end of the talk she asks if there are any questions. Many times in my past my Self-talk has been something like this: "If I ask my question, I will sound stupid, and I will be embarrassed. I am afraid to ask my question, so I will not".

Now, because I was prone to feel that way, I have changed my Self-talk to this: "I am going to raise my hand with confidence and ask a very interesting question. The speaker and others present will also find it interesting."

There have been times when I have had to enter a restaurant by myself-one I have never been in. I used to say something like this: "I might mess up and go in the wrong direction, making myself look foolish and inadequate". Now I breathe deep and say things as "I will have no trouble finding my way. If I need help, someone will be happy to set me straight. I am relaxed and enjoying this adventure."

These examples document that I am, first of all, conscious of my Self-talk. I am monitoring my words and my thoughts by taking control of my thinking and determining what I am saying to myself. I think of myself as the one in charge.

One insightful thought that Shad Helmstetter offers in his book is "The situation is outside of you; how you respond is inside of you. We might say that we have a choice to use conscious action or to use unconscious reaction." That is one powerful quote!! I am emphasizing that we should monitor what we say to ourselves internally. We should consciously control what we think; take charge of our Self-talk.

You have misplaced your shoes. You don't know where they are and you have to leave for an appointment. What are you going to say to yourself? Are you going to allow yourself to be negative, destructive in what you tell yourself, or will you take a few deep breaths, calm yourself, and say things like, "I am at peace. I will find my shoes. I will calmly look for them."

Picture yourself in line at the post office. You may be thinking negative thoughts and feeling very impatient. The option would be to check your Self-talk and, instead of saying all kinds of negative words, relax, and plan what you might do tonight. Many times I have learned to think about and review a book I am reading; or think about what I want to accomplish with my time tomorrow. The point is that our Self-talk should be productive, controlled, and valuable, not negative and destructive.

I recommend the use of Situational Self-talk to monitor our thinking, to control our thoughts, and to direct them in a positive and beneficial manner.

BOYS WITHOUT VISION URINATING

In 2005 Laura and I were happy to be at the graduation party of the son of one of my former students. At some point during the afternoon, I was having an interesting and private conversation with Dennis, my former student. He made a stimulating comment. He kindly said that there was one thing Ralph and I did not teach him. Dennis was referring to Ralph who, with his wife Delores, was the originator of the 1955 educational program for the blind in River Rouge, Michigan. Dennis had been in the first group of students. Not surprisingly, I asked Dennis what it was that we had missed. This is what he told me!

"You never taught me how to pee properly." He said we should have shown him how to touch his knees to the front of the toilet and thereby be sure that his urine would flow straight into the toilet as opposed to being on an angle and urinating partially on the floor.

I have thought about that quite a bit since that stimulating discussion. It's such an easy technique to be sure your aim is accurate, but as I think about it, no one ever explained or discussed this with me either. I remembered as a young boy making mistakes myself.

In the early 1980s I had an adventurous student teacher named Joel. One night Joel decided to function without sight; he put on a blindfold for the evening. The next day he told me how he urinated, but failed to line up properly and went on the floor. I wonder why I did not think more about that, and instruct my students to perform the simple technique of just touching the toilet bowl with their knees to make sure they were lined up properly.

I have included this story because the action is so important, and yet to my knowledge, it is not taught to youngsters. By the way, it is thrilling to me that Dennis has had a wonderful life and is now retired. (He must somehow be older than me!) He graciously read each chapter in this book and gave me his suggestions and feedback—except this one. Wait until he reads it!!!

DREAMING

The kind of dreams I'm referring to are not about the dreams that take place during sleep. I'm talking about the dreams we have about our lives, our futures, and what we hope to achieve.

I think parents and teachers should take time to encourage young people to have dreams about their lives. A third grade teacher friend of mine told me that several of his students told him that they had dreamed of one day being a professional hockey player. He said he firmly told them to forget such an impossible dream; their chances of becoming a professional hockey player are almost impossible. I personally believe that he should have, with enthusiasm, supported and encouraged each one of them to keep that dream alive and work toward it. It is wonderful to have dreams and goals whether you are young or old. My sincere advice to everyone is to dream away and enjoy the dream. That is not to say that we will always achieve our dreams, but the inspiration, the joy, and the motivation they give are valuable. My poem called DREAM, from my book <u>DIE DAILY</u>, says in twelve lines exactly what I am writing about.

"DREAM"

My advice to myself and maybe you'll agree,
Is to DIE daily; it'll set you free!
It's a three-letter word, the first letter is D.
The D stands for dream. Please listen to me.

Take time to dream every single day,
That's so important, that's what I say!
So take time to dream, it will enrich your life,
Let your mind soar, take time out from strife,

Take time each day to put your head in a cloud,
Of this time you can surely be proud,
Dream away and don't delay,
This should be part of our every day!

My purpose is to convey the importance of dreaming because it can motivate a person to achieve, to live with enthusiasm, and to put to full use their God-given abilities.

TACTILE DRAWINGS

Pictures are an integral part of life for people with vision. Pictures can say a lot, stimulate interest, and add pleasure to living. This is rarely part of life for people who cannot see. My hope is that this will change in the near future, and there will be tactile pictures in Braille books and on Braille book covers. One of my dreams is that every Braille book at the National Library Service for the Blind would have an appealing tactile picture on the cover. I have had the joy of producing four of my DIE DAILY books into Braille, and every cover has a tactile picture of the sun shining.

There is a significant difference between visual pictures and tactile pictures. Last year my brother Frank and I produced a booklet called Marvelous Michigan. Frank took on the challenge of thinking tactually with me. Realize that Frank sees pictures with his eyes, and always has, so he thinks visually. I see with my fingers, and so I think tactually. It required a significant alteration of his thinking to accomplish our task and I commend him for that. Three maps of Michigan were included in the booklet. Frank's assignment was to simplify the pictures so that the sense of touch would be the means through which there would be an understanding of the items in the picture.

For starters, the amount of detail in the tactile drawings needs to be reduced in comparison to a visual picture. Secondly, tactile pictures should be spacious. Each item in the picture needs to be sized large enough to make it easy for fingers to comprehend. Words used to label pictures should be spaced apart not jammed, on the page, to be comfortable to read. Included in Chapter 7 are three tactile pictures I made which are duplicated from tactile drawings. They are a football field, a baseball diamond, and bowling lane.

Ideally, every blind child could experience a football field if they were taken there to walk the length of the field, yard by yard, and then to walk the entire fifty three and one third yard width of the field. The person doing this could help the student explore the end zone, including the goal post structure. Doing that would develop a good internal picture of a football field. The same can be said about a baseball diamond, bowling lanes and many other venues.

My mind flows with rich, wonderful memories of having real experiences with sports as a boy, thanks to my sensational brothers Frank and Cecil who involved me in every sport they played. In baseball they rolled the ball on the ground for me to hear and then I'd hit. Besides batting, in order for me to fully participate, they often had me be the pitcher. I was so fortunate to have Frank and Cecil. They made sure I was part of everything we did in our neighborhood. I was accepted for who I was, and adaptations were made so that I was totally included.

In the 1990s, I was giving Mona and Shannon, my fifth graders, the Michigan Educational Assessment Test. The section they were working on was science, and the question had to do with the solar system. They had to feel "raised line drawings" to answer the questions. They became frustrated because they could make absolutely no sense out of the tactile drawing. I tried to help them figure it out, but I, too, was totally frustrated. My colleague and friend Margaret Navarro happened to walk in. I asked her if she could make sense out of the picture. The fantastic part of this story is that Margaret took a quick glance and immediately knew what the picture was all about. I tell this incident because first, it really amazes me how marvelous eyes are, and second, how pictures cannot be duplicated from visual pictures to tactile pictures.

PUTTING HAND ON CHAIR BACK

A simple, easy, and efficient way for someone to show a blind person where a chair is for them to sit is to just put the blind person's hand on the back of the chair.

So often, when someone shows a blind person to their chair, they will say, "Just to your left." That's plenty of information if one can see, but so much is not communicated to one who is blind—is the chair straight left, how far left, which way does it face or is it forward or back? Those who are blind should say to the person showing them to a chair, "Just put my hand on the back of the chair." That says it all.

STUDY SKILLS

This part of the chapter is aimed primarily at high school students preparing for college.

I believe that a Study Skills class should be a part of the school curriculum.

I speak from experience, realizing how totally ill-prepared I was for Michigan State College. Incidentally, I started as a freshman at Michigan State College, but due to their name change, I graduated from Michigan State University. I am so grateful to my professors for their tolerance and commitment to helping me to be successful in spite of being unprepared.

The following list names the topics that would be included in a Study Skills class.

- Developing Memory Skills. Basically students would be taught to use the three R's—recognizing, retaining, and retrieving. This would involve such important features as pegging, acronyms, visualizing, and having hands-on experiences. The last two, hands-on experience and visualizing, are especially vital.
- Learning Creative Thinking or "thinking outside the box." I think this is important for everyone, but if you cannot see, or have low vision, thinking outside the box is especially good to learn because you do not learn exactly like sighted people.
- Being Competent with Braille. Braille is vital if you are blind or have minimal vision. The process is a different way of learning. It is similar to learning to read with your eyes, but you learn with your fingers.

- <u>Developing Listening Skills</u>. Not everything a student is faced with will be in Braille, so auditory skills are also necessary. Students should be taught how to learn in an auditory manner. They will be listening to compact discs and to people reading to them. They need to be competent in listening and develop that skill for use in lectures, class reviews, and taking notes.
- <u>Typing Effectively</u>. Students will need to be competent in basic typing, including formatting of print documents.
- <u>Writing Papers for College Classes</u>. Preparation for writing acceptably the footnotes, endnotes, bibliography, and references.
- <u>Note Taking and Reviewing</u>. The content would include an introduction and familiarity with the various methods and pieces of equipment to facilitate this skill.

STUDYING WITH OTHERS

Studying with others is a great learning activity. The next experience illustrates the point. During my college years at Michigan State there were no textbooks written in Braille, nor were any books recorded on computer disks. There were no computers. The only way any blind student had to read textbooks was through the kindness of volunteers who read to us. The girl who read to me in the fall of 1953 was Mary Adams. I nicknamed her "Stony. She read to me once a week all Fall Term, and we developed a good friendship. When it came time to sign up for Winter Term classes, we agreed to take a history class together. We made a verbal contract that we would study together, and we both would get an "A" in the class. We attended class together, of course, and after class we discussed the ideas, concepts, and facts that were presented. It was helpful to clarify our own and each other's thinking. We also read the textbook together. We didn't just read it, but discussed what was presented.

The class was a big success for us. We both got an "A" in the class, as planned, but we also learned a great deal and enjoyed studying together. Michigan State was on a three term schedule, so Spring Term we took a GENEALOGY class. Interestingly, at that time

Michigan State had 3 ten-week terms—fall, winter, spring. We were just as successful in the GENEALOGY class as we had been in the history class.

To give this section of the book a human touch, I will mention that 55 years later, in 2008, Stony and I had lunch together. We talked fondly about the two classes we had taken together and how meaningful they had been. By the way, let me explain the name "Stony". During the first two weeks that Mary read to me, she got a cold. Her voice sounded like she had gravel in her throat. No, I did not nickname her "Gravel"; I nicknamed her "Stony". To me, she still is Stony, and she said she likes the name.

Now I have something important to tell you. Stony and I did not sit down after class and discuss the lessons. We should have, and I wish we had. What I said above is what I wish we had done. There now, I've told you the truth!

Had I learned in high school how valuable studying with someone is, it could have opened an important door for me in college. Studying together might be something a new student would want to try.

BRAIN STORMING

I have included this topic because I believe it is an important technique. It can lead to many good ideas, activities, and solutions to problems.

Brainstorming can be done alone, which I call "personal brainstorming", or with others in a group setting. The example here describes what I would do using brainstorming alone. It starts with my having a problem to deal with, or a situation that I need to take care of. In this case, I want to do something recreational tomorrow, something just for fun. I just need a break, but I really don't know quite what I would like to do, so I make a list of possible activities. I set no boundaries or limits to my thinking. I let my mind fly freely. My list might look like this:

- Play golf with a friend
- Take a bus ride some place
- Sleep in a tent in the backyard tonight
- Fly to the moon

Here's the point—I am not evaluating my ideas as I make my list; I will do that later. A good question is "Why in heck would I put down 'fly to the moon'?" I can't do that! Remember, when brainstorming, any idea is acceptable and encouraged. There are absolutely no limits.

After the brainstorming session, I go back to the list and start my evaluation of the ideas. Now I notice the idea of flying to the moon, and I think about what a great adventure it would be to take an air balloon flight. Incidentally, my idea to fly to the moon resulted in my actually taking my grandchildren on a hot air balloon ride. It is confirmation for me that something that appears to be a wild idea on a brainstorm list may evolve into a meaningful event. In addition, keep in mind that brainstorming is fun and exciting to do.

GOAL SETTING

All of us, but I think especially young people, should take time to think about goals, set goals, and then work at achieving those goals. Earlier in this chapter I discussed the importance of dreams. Although they are not the same, it seems to me that in order to achieve a dream, a person must set goals and work toward those goals.

The importance of goal setting came to my attention when I listened to a presentation by a very interesting man who told about an incident that happened when he was 15 years old. He was busy doing things in the kitchen at home. There was a group of adults talking in the living room, discussing things they wished they had done earlier in their lives. The subject caught the boy's attention. He said to himself, "I don't want to be sitting and talking thirty or forty years from now about what I wish *I* had done during my life". Then he started writing down goals that he wanted to achieve during his life. I believe he had something like 110 goals. Then he started to work on them.

I'm not recommending that we all establish that many goals, but I am recommending that we do think about and pursue important goals that we want to accomplish. Again, I wish I had been led in this direction as a boy or a young man.

Now, for a personal story, I heard a gentleman speak on goal setting in March 1984. The next day I was running outside, working at keeping physically fit. My mind was free flowing, when all of a sudden it struck me—what if I set a goal to run a marathon? Until that moment, not in my wildest dreams had it ever occurred to me that I could do something even close to running a marathon.

I set that goal, trained for it, and achieved it the following October by running The Detroit Free Press Marathon. My finish time was five hours and eleven minutes. Relatively speaking that's very slow, but that's not the point. Rather, it was the fact that just a few months earlier, I would not even have thought that was possible, and yet here I was achieving, what was for me, an unbelievable goal. In order for me to make my goal happen I had the help of three friends—Nina, Bob, and Mike, who each ran a leg of the marathon with me. Without their participation and encouragement I could not have done it. My thanks went out to them at the time, and still does today, for helping me make my goal a reality.

When I got into goal setting in the 80's, I included my 4th, 5th, and 6th grade students. We discussed what goal setting is, and that if they wanted to they could set three goals for the school year. I explained that those who worked at and achieved their goals by June would be rewarded with a lunch at Portofino's. This is a restaurant in Wyandotte where people can be seated on the deck at the edge of the Detroit River. The students achieved their goals. It was a culminating activity to an exciting year. I wish you well if you choose to have goals, and if you decide to set and work toward those goals.

PHYSICAL FITNESS

In 1981, my daughter Marla, age 14, came to me and asked if I'd go with her to the bank so she could cash her check. I told her that I'd be glad to go with her, but we'd have to run because the bank was closing in five minutes. We started running and within 50 feet I was totally beat. I simply had to stop running; I could not go any farther. That's how unfit I was. I realized that I should not live in such an unhealthy manner. I knew it was not good for my body, brain, or mind. That's when I started working out.

My recommendation is to work out just three times per week. Doing so will keep your body and mind fit. Going out for just a 20-30 minute walk three times per week is a good fitness activity and is not an overly demanding commitment compared to the benefits.

MAKE LEARNING FUN. MAKE LIFE FUN

This book is about living, learning, and loving. We all could live life fully and happily.

If we are living fully, learning will always be a part of our lives. We would be joyfully loving life, loving ourselves, and loving one another. I hope that makes positive sense.

Chapter Summary

The summary for this chapter is my poem, 86,400

86,400

What in the world could this number be for?
I hope it's not someone's golfing score!
Or let's hope it's not how much I weigh,
For golf I would not be able to play!

Let us think in the direction of time.
Hopefully you'll find much reason and rhyme.
In the math that I will express,
So off we go! We will not digress!

There are 24 hours in every day,
In which we can work, sleep and play,
We can dream, and think, and cogitate,
Let's try to make each hour great!

In every hour 60 minutes are given,
Let's make each minute a moment for livin',
There are 1440 minutes per day,
Let's take each minute to swing and sway!

I'm sure you know that we're not yet done,
There's one more step and it's kind of fun.
Get ready to use your lively mind,
This will be exciting, I'm sure you'll find!

60 seconds in every minute—you bet!
60 times 1440 and what do we get?
Why not stop right here and calculate,
A five-digit number will be your fate!

86,400 seconds per day,
A truly exciting figure I'd say.
You can count them—it's up to you,
As for me I've got other things to do!

Let's give each second our very best,
If we do, our life will surely be blessed,
Each second is a gift from Heaven above,
Fill it with life! Fill it with love!

We have 24 hours every day,
1440 minutes you say,
86,400 seconds hurray!
Let's go out—live and not delay!

In 2009 my poetry book, <u>DIE DAILY</u>, was published. The title might shock you! Who in the world wants to Die Daily? Guess what! That is what I try to do. I try my best to Die Daily—that is, I try my best to:

DREAM, IMPROVE, ENJOY.

The "D" means I dream about my life and set goals.

The "I" means I work to improve myself all the time.

The "E" is for enjoy. I pay attention to enjoying my life.

Thus: I try my best to dream, to improve, and to enjoy each day.

At any given time in my life I hope I did my best, but I plan to be better tomorrow than I am today. I aim to dream, to improve, and to enjoy each moment.

Chapter Humor

Question: When is it correct to add eleven plus two, and get the answer "one"?

****

Answer: If it is eleven o'clock and you add two hours it will be one o'clock. In this case, eleven plus two equals one!!

CHAPTER 13

PLEASANT PLEA TO PARENTS

To parents this is my plea,
Please feel free to disagree!

This chapter is meant to pull together the ideas I have presented. It is a review of the entire book. In Chapters 1-3, I encourage teaching students with low or no vision to be proud of who they are. Parents can play an important role in motivating their children to enjoy being their unique and unlimited selves. Every youngster should be taught to focus on their abilities and to be comfortable with themselves, and consequently, help others to be comfortable with them. (I am emphasizing the word COMFORTABLE). Moreover, I would recommend that we keep improving, and while improving, enjoy each moment we live.

Avoid having a child perceive that if a person has low vision, or is blind, that that is something to be ashamed of. Each youngster should be proud of who they are. Everyone should focus on developing their abilities and have the adventure and fun of achievement.

Finally, Self-talk, as taught by Shad Helmstetter, is so vital that we all should freely use Self-Talk about others and ourselves. We should keep our Self-talk positive, and employ "SITUATIONAL Self-talk" as described by Shad Helmstetter throughout the day.

Children with low vision, or no vision, should start developing orientation skills early in life. Parents and teachers should ensure that they learn not to be afraid to be mobile, but rather to think of it as an adventure. We need to encourage all of the skills talked about in <u>Chapter 5</u>: the value of using a white cane, a leader dog, and global positioning devices. In fact, with much enthusiasm, I want to tell you that I bought a new GPS device called Breeze. I am presently learning how to use it as I walk or ride in a car.

In <u>Chapter 6</u> I talk about learning "directional orientation" including map and compass directions and numbers on a face clock.

<u>Chapter 7</u> encourages the use of visualization (mental pictures) and acoustics (sound waves) for greater mobility.

In <u>Chapter 8</u> I make a plea for parents to read to their youngsters. While reading together, I recommend discussing the reading and the ideas and words in the book. Registration with the National Library Service for the Blind is one way to obtain Braille books, magazines, and music resources. I strongly advocate the idea of drawing simple tactile pictures to go along with the reading.

In <u>Chapter 9</u> there is a discussion of writing, with the proper fingering, on a Qwerty and Perkins style Braillewriter. I stress the importance of children learning how to write their name in print, using pen and pencil. Another tool that can be used in writing is the slate and stylus.

<u>Chapters 10 and 11</u> introduces you to available screen readers, screen magnifiers, and notetakers; websites and phone numbers are included.

In <u>Chapter 12</u>, I encourage parents to provide lots and lots of hands-on experiences. I use the metaphor that people with low or no vision "see with their fingers". Although during my life I did have ample hands-on experience, I wish I had understood how important hands-on experience is. The exciting part is that as I make the effort to "see with my fingers", people get involved. For example, my friend Nina invited me to a small musical concert. Before the program began, we walked onto the stage so I could touch the music stands and the placement of the chairs, as well as the piano and the drum set. Knowing that ahead of time made the sounds more meaningful. to have a great experience.

Here's another story! Please think about what I'm conveying. I am now 78 years of age. On the 4th of July, I was invited for dinner with my friends—John and Arlene. John and I went out onto the back porch to grill the T-bone steaks. John showed me my T-bone steak. I felt it with interest. For the first time in 78 years, I know what is meant by T-bone steak. The bone forms an imperfect letter "T" within the steak. Can you believe that for 78 years I had no idea why it is called a T-bone steak? I thought it was just a crazy, meaningless name.

I had an additional hands-on experience with my steak. I did the grilling myself. That, too, was an adventure. I tell this story because it underscores, at least for me, the profound value of learning through touch.

Finally, in <u>Chapter 12</u>, I offer power-boosting thoughts and suggestions to build one's effectiveness and confidence. These include deep breathing, self-talk, brainstorming, study skills, and goals.

In today's world of computers, children who have low vision or who are blind definitely need to be skilled in their use. I strongly recommend that those with low vision use a screen magnification program. (See <u>Chapter 10</u>). Those who are blind need to learn the skills for using a Braille computer usually referred to as a Braille notetaker. They should also be familiar with a screen reader with speech. Computers with Braille, speech, and screen magnification should be readily available for all at home and school.

CHAPTER HUMOR:

Question: What do you get when a turtle and a porcupine unite?

****

Answer: A slow poke!

A concluding thought to end this book.

When a man was asked how he felt about losing his sight, he replied, "It doesn't really matter, I've just lost my sight but not my vision."

BIBLIOGRAPHY

Helmstetter, Shad. *What to Say When You Talk to Yourself.* New York: Pocket, 1987. Print.

Lennox, Ted, and Nina Derda. *Die Daily: Dream, Improve, Enjoy.* [S.l.]: Trafford, 2009. Print.

Lennox, Ted, Anna Dresner, and Katy Snyder. *A Simple Guide to Word for Kids.* Boston, MA: National Braille, 2004. Print.

Lucaweicki, Viola. *Daily Word:* Reality. Jan. 1975. Print.

Recommended References

American Printing House for the Blind. Web. 01 Oct. 2011. <http://www.aph.org>.

The American Printing House has a beginning typing program called Talking Typer. They also have slates and styluses. Here is the contact information: www.aph.org>. Phone: 1-800 231-1839.

Curran, Eileen P. *Just Enough to Know Better: A Braille Primer.* Boston, MA: National Braille, 2010. Print.

For parents and teachers, this self-paced workbook teaches you just enough Braille to read along with your child. Here is the contact information with many editions to choose from: phone: 800 548-7323. The cost is less than $10.00.

"Home Page of the National Library Service for the Blind and Physically Handicapped." *Library of Congress Home*. Web. 29 Sep. 2011. <http://www.loc.gov/nls/>.

Lennox, Laura and Ted. Beginning Braille Kit. 01 Apr. 1976.

This small kit is an easy introduction to basic Braille, which teaches the letters of the alphabet for reading and writing Braille. It includes an inexpensive plastic slate and a stylus. Kits are available via Ted Lennox by phone at 313 846-0318.

NBP—Promoting Braille Literacy, Braille Books, and Other Braille Publications. Web. 14 Oct. 2011.

The National Braille Press is an excellent organization that provides books for children and adults. I am recommending the Print and Braille combined books for children. I am especially referencing the Learning Beginning Braille, which is a book for parents. The URL is ww.nbp.org>.

Seedlings Braille Books for Children. Web. 22 Sep. 2011.

Seedlings has wonderful Braille books for children to read. They also have books for parents and children to read together. Those meant for both parents and children are in both Braille and print. They have a Braille kit entitled Hurray for Braille. It is aimed at teaching Braille basics to parents, teachers, and others. Here is the contact information: info@seedlings.org. Phone number: (734)-427-8552.